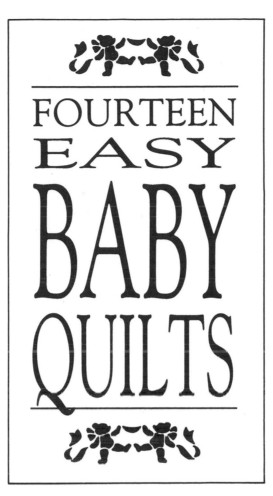

FOURTEEN EASY BABY QUILTS

Other books in the Contemporary Quilting series,
available from Chilton

Fast Patch: A Treasury of Strip-Pieced Quilts, by
    Anita Hallock
Speed-Cut Quilts, by Donna Poster

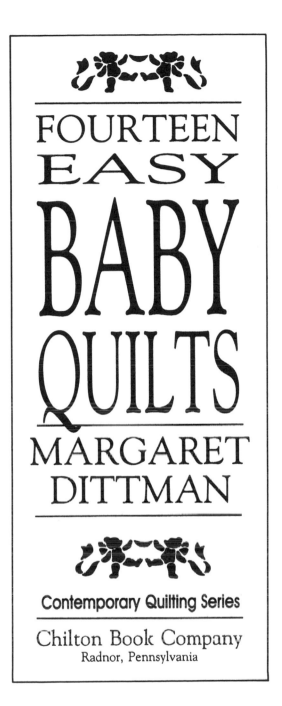

FOURTEEN EASY BABY QUILTS

MARGARET DITTMAN

Contemporary Quilting Series

Chilton Book Company

Radnor, Pennsylvania

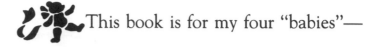This book is for my four "babies"—

Michael Cooper,
Lacy Dittman,
Samarra Dittman,
and
Evan Dittman.

Protected trademarks used in this book are:

Dual Duty Plus®
Ensure® Quilt Wash
Hot Stitch™
Polaroid®
Polydown-DK®
Q-Snap™
Teflon®
Ultrasuede®
Warm & Natural™
Wonder-Under® Transfer Fusing Web

Designed by Anthony Jacobson
Manufactured in the United States of America

Library of Congress Cataloging in Publication Data
Dittman, Margaret.
    Fourteen easy baby quilts / Margaret Dittman.
      p. cm.—(Contemporary quilting)
    Includes index.
    ISBN 0-8019-8027-5 (pbk.)
    1. Quilting—Patterns. 2. Patchwork—Patterns. 3. Children's
quilts. I. Title. II. Title: 14 easy baby quilts. III. Series.
TT835.D58   1990
746.9'7—dc20
                                     90-55322
                                       CIP

1 2 3 4 5 6 7 8 9 0   0 9 8 7 6 5 4 3 2 1

FOREWORD

Known fact: Quilters have enough fabric right now to make a quilt for each person in the entire world. By next month, there will be enough to start on back-up quilts. (However, there are still quilters out there who are short on purples.)

How has this happened? The answers tumble out faster than I can follow them. Piecework started out to be a functional and frugal art. *Frugal* is the key word here. It's the word all quilters lean on. It makes us feel sensible and mature. Actually, we're self-indulgent and like to play a lot. Cliches fit us to a T: "Make a silk purse out of a sow's ear," "Use it up, wear it out, make it do," "Idle hands do the devil's work," and a hundred more. *Functional* means we do not waste our time on frivolous things. Ah, but *our* functional things encompass so much. . . .

It all starts with a little itch that grows into a Desire and then into a MAD NEED TO MAKE SOMETHING! Ideas, plans, more grandiose plans and then *acquisition of materials*! We love the hunting out and buying of fabrics. This is the gregarious part. Next, we get to handle it, look at it, store it, look at it some more—this is the private part. Then we get to use it, actually play with it, cut it up, put it back together, and make our something. This is the personal part. Finally, after all this, we *still* have it to share with someone—back to being gregarious. Sure beats spending money on nouvelle cuisine!

Inspiration is continually coming at us from all directions: nature, music, poetry, man-made structures, memories, dreams and love. But it's quilting books of all kinds that help us to finalize our concepts, teach us new techniques, and build our confidence. Because of this, we *must* be grateful to authors who actually sit themselves down and *write out* pages in finished form for publishers to print.

How else would we keep from flying apart?

Mary Ellen Hopkins
Santa Monica, California
October, 1990

CONTENTS

PREFACE

What if you're not at all crafty, but your only sister is expecting her first baby and you have an overwhelming desire to make a baby quilt? What if your sewing skills are limited to hemming jeans and sewing on buttons? What can you do?

Answer: Read this book. You'll find directions for over a dozen easy baby quilts and ideas for many more. Even if you've never sewn before, you'll be inspired to mark the occasion with a handmade gift. And your inspiration is a popular one—even the rustiest needle fingers get to itching when a new baby's on the way. Making things for Christmas runs only a distant second in evoking creativity, and there are no other contenders in the field. Clothing for babies is hard to make, with all those tiny seams and curves. Let the little darlings wear store-bought cotton-knit gowns while you put all your love and energy into something fast, easy, and impressive. The impact of a baby quilt is large, indeed. Babies can actually bond with their quilts.

Shortly after my niece Cory was born, I made her a sweet little quilt, all lace, rose-patterned prints, and pastels. Rather than quilt it by hand (are you *kidding*?), I tied it strategically here and there with pink yarn ties. The quilt soon assumed magical proportions in Cory's life. It acquired a name—"Rosie"—and a new verb came into being. *To rosie* was to fondle the soft little balls the yarn ties formed after several washings. *To rosie* was an absolutely required prelude to falling asleep. By the time Cory was seven years old, poor old "Rosie" was in dire straits, with some fabric squares absolutely vacant. Because I'd used fabrics with different fiber contents, some squares had

just disintegrated, while others had more or less kept the quilt's structural integrity intact. Cory wrote me a letter on the family's word processor:

Dear Aunt Margaret:
    Will you make me a new Rosie?

This is the fuel for the quilter's fire. Not only had this child loved, hugged, and appreciated her gift—which hadn't taken more than six or eight pleasant hours to make—she had also requested a replacement. I was delighted to fill her request. I even found scraps of some of the same fabrics I'd used in the original. (I hope they weren't the same ones that disintegrated.) Both old and new Rosies are shown in Figure 1 in the color section in this book.

You can make a baby quilt, believe me. And baby quilts have enormous importance in a child's life. If you don't have babies in your immediate circle, you'll find great satisfaction in giving a quilt to a local charity hospital, orphanage, or women's shelter (see Chapter 19). Besides, these quilts don't have to be for babies only. The designs in this book will appeal to babies, little kids, big kids, the inner child, and the wild child. These quilts can be for wrap, lap, or nap. You can make most of these quilts in a few hours, employing your present level of sewing skill and possibly using fabric scraps and notions you already have on hand. Measuring and mathematics are kept to a minimum. If you're looking for pastel puppies and cute little clowns, you'll probably want to put this book back on the shelf. Oh, we've got some puppies, all right—and dinosaurs, too—but mostly you'll find snappy, modern, artsy quilt designs with big visual impact and few patterns. These quilts will be fun for you to make, and they're sure to please, comfort, and stimulate the lucky baby recipients far more than "traditional" baby quilts would. We're not talking fussy little appliqués or precise patchwork here; we're going to make quilts that can be washed, rolled on, rosied on, wagged around, and *loved*.

ACKNOWLEDGMENTS

Except where noted otherwise, the black-and-white photographs in this book are by John Anglim; color photography is by Anglim & Childress. Illustrations throughout are by Charlie Davis-Young, who also served as our hand model.

For supplying materials aided in researching this book, I'd like to thank the Tacony Corporation; the Viking White Company; Fairfield Processing Corporation; Concord Fabrics, Inc.; Aardvark Adventures in Handcrafts; June Tailor, Inc.; Metrosene Thread; Speed Stitch; Wamsutta Fabrics; and Clotilde, Inc.

Thanks also to our models, Kay and Adrian Leitch and Austin Childress.

And thanks to Robbie Fanning, who one day remarked, "All my friends are having babies. I need a book on making baby quilts. I've got a title but no author. Are you game?" Now who can resist bait like that!

INTRODUCTION WHO IS THIS WOMAN, ANYWAY?

I introduced myself to a young man in an art gallery, and I told him I made quilts and garments. "Ah," he answered, "Nimble fingers, huh?" And after I'd thought about it, I said, "No, I'm a klutz. I just love doing it. Imagine Inspector Clouseau at the quilt frame."

I'm not going to suggest that we do anything remotely difficult to make baby quilts. If I can do the things in this book, so can you. Although I'm in my forties and have been making little quilts for years, no one could stretch her imagination far enough to call me an accomplished quilter.

What I am accomplished in is having fun, making things, and writing. In addition to raising children (and silkworms, goats, chickens, cats, and the like), I've edited needlecraft magazines (*Needle & Thread, Needlecraft for Today,* and *Needle & Craft*). The best aspect of the magazine job, aside from the travel, was the opportunity to meet hundreds of accomplished artists and craftspeople—including the best quilters. I also wrote *The Fabric Lover's Scrapbook,* published by Chilton Book Company in 1988.

So that I don't have to use parentheses and long explanations, let me first introduce you to my cast of characters and to one highly technical term used in this book.

Ma: My grandmother, a prolific folk artist. Delpha Anne Elizabeth Taylor was her real name, but everybody called her Annie. I lived with her throughout my early childhood, and she was a major influence on my quiltmaking and other important areas of life. Pa, of course, was her husband and my beloved grandfather.

Golda: My mother, who is a marvelous seamstress. A few years ago I decided to alter our relationship subtly by calling her by her first name. (I recommend this, by the way, to those of you who have outworn the old mother-daughter pathways.)

Fred: My husband of 20 years, who thinks all the thread and lint around the place are quite picturesque.

Michael, Lacy, and Marra: Kids who are grown and gone.

Evan: The last kid left at home. By the time you read this, I may have moved more fabric and sewing machines into his vacated room.

Charlie: Charlie Davis, my long-time friend, coeditor, traveling companion, and illustrator. (Yes, Charlie is a woman.)

Trash fabric: Fabric that will disappear *inside* a quilt. It can be old or new, muslin or cotton flannel, the kitchen curtains or some yardage you never should have bought in the first place. It should retain its structural integrity (not be in rags and tatters), and it should not be loosely woven or stretchy. It can even be an ugly, lime-green cotton with large orange flowers unless it's going to show through a delicate white print. Trash fabric should have a high preponderance of natural fibers—cotton, preferably. Linen is usually pretty ravelly; wool is all right if it is preshrunk completely and is closely woven.

CHAPTER ONE
THE PLANNING STAGES

The Quilter

Do you want this to be a long-term project or a quickie project? Do you like to sew by hand or on the sewing machine? Do you easily become frustrated, or are you proud of your patience? Do you want to learn something new or to relax with familiar techniques?

These are all questions about *you*. If you've tried cross-stitch embroidery and weren't too thrilled with it, don't embark on a cross-stitched quilt no matter how much you like the design. If you have never made a quilt before and you have a tendency to toss troublesome projects into the Goodwill bag, you'll want to choose a quilt that's quick and easy.

The Parents

The parents of your quilt's intended recipient may not be an important factor to you, or this consideration might be first on your list. The quilt is, after all, for the baby, not for the grown-ups. However, since they can't very well be separated, let's consider the parents.

With what styles are the parents comfortable? If you know for a fact that your sister hates green, you'll probably decide to keep green to a minimum in your color scheme. If the happy couple maintains a new-wave, high-tech apartment, don't make their new baby a multiflowered Victorian lace coverlet (unless they're showing signs of getting mushy themselves—it happens.)

Are the parents perfectionists? Again, having a baby changes people enormously, and per-

fectionism is one of the first casualties of parenthood. If the new mom and dad are picky, though, you might elect to make a very easy quilt in which all the pieces will match and lie flat, rather than a folk-art piece with ripples, tucks, and unexpected colors. Then again, you never can tell. If the parents think your quilt isn't all that perfect and desirable, they may let the baby use it for "everyday" instead of keeping it "nice." And this, after all, is what we want. You'll have to decide for yourself what approach to take, based on your perceptions of the parents.

Where does the family live and in what style? For a Montana ranch baby, choose durable and washable fabrics and strong construction techniques—in other words, make a tough quilt. A baby in New Orleans doesn't need heavy woolens and thick batting. Of course, today's families are known for their mobility, so the geographical and cultural consideration may not assume much importance in your plans. You'll probably want to think about these things, however, before you take scissors in hand.

The Actual Quilt

Everybody plans a quilt differently, but the planning generally goes something like this:

1. Energy, impulse, idea
2. Thoughts of the recipient
3. Mental image of shapes and colors
4. Pulling (choosing) fabric
5. Pattern or technique
6. Narrowing your choices

The first two phases are self-explanatory. You think, "Hey, I'll make a quilt for Brenda's new baby," and you've breezed right through steps 1 and 2.

Now it's time to form a *mental image* of this quilt-to-be. If an idea of the overall effect doesn't come to you immediately, you can meditate on the parents, what the baby might be like, family history, how you felt when you were expecting a child, images from nature, and life in general. This very book in your hands can be a wellspring of images and ideas. There are books and magazines listed at the end of this book to serve in that same capacity. If the images still don't appear, go on to step 4. Fabric is often a splendid spur to the imagination.

Choosing fabric is such a personal matter that it's hard to address. One of my favorite role models, Mary Ellen Hopkins, has a saying: "Don't get dressed when you're pulling fabric." She doesn't mean to design in your underwear, but to be brave and toss in some startling fabric, fabric you wouldn't include in your daily wardrobe mix. Safe color and fabric choices make boring quilts. We've all seen too many of them—nice little beige or light-blue calico numbers, usually. I may be prejudiced, but we artsy quilters like a little shock in the design, and psychologists believe that babies do, too.

Where do you go to find your fabric? Either you've been sewing awhile and have a collection, or you don't. Maybe some stitcher you know will give you all her scraps, or maybe you will have to go to the fabric store.

Now I have some good news and some bad

news about the fabric store. The good news is that stitchers are happy to share what they know. You are welcome to take as much time as you like, fondle the fabrics to your heart's content, and change your mind a hundred times before the clerk starts to cut. The most experienced stitchers do this, so you won't be at all out of place. The bad news is that a lot of people freeze up when confronted by the plethora of polyester, the cacaphony of cottons, the fusillade of flannels. Too much stuff. It's hard to start.

My advice is to start with something you already own and like. If you're not a stitcher and don't have a fabric collection, don't worry. You probably have a skirt you loved before you gained those 10 pounds or a tablecloth and no table. Hey, it's OK. Fabric does not have to come from the fabric store. I buy lots of fabric at the Goodwill store. Oh, it's not labeled fabric; it's like-new size 18 cotton dresses, huge gathered linen skirts, roomy caftans, silk evening gowns that took 10 yards to make. You get the idea. Of course you'll wash it when you get it home; there aren't going to be any germs clinging to it. If you're brave and opinionated, of course you can start cold in the fabric store. Most of us, however, need a color scheme firmly in mind before we set foot inside the doors of those palaces of choice.

If the circumstances are right, ask the new mother to contribute a few pieces of fabric. One of my favorite quilts has some bits of rayon pajamas that Golda wore when I was a toddler. Looking at the mailbox-and-hearts print, I am once again sitting on her lap while she reads. The quilt has bits of silky dresses Ma wore to church; those bits evoke the scent of cloves she'd tuck into her purse, later into her mouth to sweeten her breath. History, in other words, can be as powerful a consideration as utility.

Sometimes you'll choose the *pattern or technique* you want to use before choosing the fabrics,

Figure 1-1. The scraps in this old quilt made by my grandmother take me right back to my first years.

sometimes afterward. The two may burst into full-blown certainty simultaneously; then you know you're on the right track.

This brings us to *narrowing your choices.* You can't do everything that tempts your fancy in one quilt. There'll be more quilts—trust me. Get serious and honest about how long you can take to make this one particular quilt. Do you really want to embroider the baby's name on every block? Wouldn't machine quilting be as effective as hand quilting? The carpenters say, "Measure twice and cut once"; quilters say, "Sleep on it, and you'll come up with a simpler idea in the morning."

Figure 1. Cory's old "Rosie" is in rags and tatters, so I made her a new one.

Figure 2. Jean Ray Laury's "Lunar Madness" is a perfect example of a sophisticated, artsy quilt made with just one size square—or is it? See Chapter 6. (Photograph courtesy of the artist.)

Figure 3. "Domenic's Quilt" is dramatic, but so easy. It's made with 8″ squares, and no frills or tricks. (Photograph courtesy of PSC Publications.)

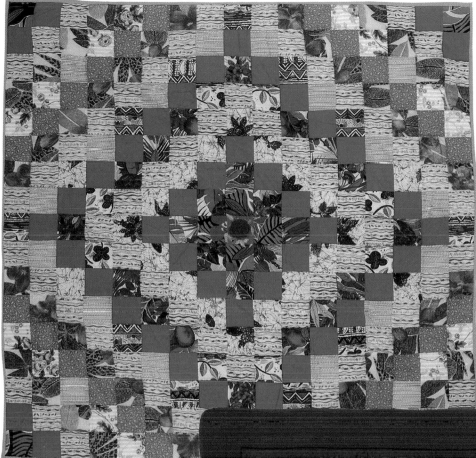

Figure 4. This simple Trip Around the World quilt is splashed with color and big tropical prints.

Figure 5. Somewhere between the Amish and the sixties, "Opti-Dots" depends on easy construction, lavish colors, and great fabrics. This quilt is silk and cotton, quilted with red silk thread.

Figure 6. This scrappy little nine-patch by Gwen Marston and Joe Cunningham is alive with color. The hand quilting puts icing on the cake.

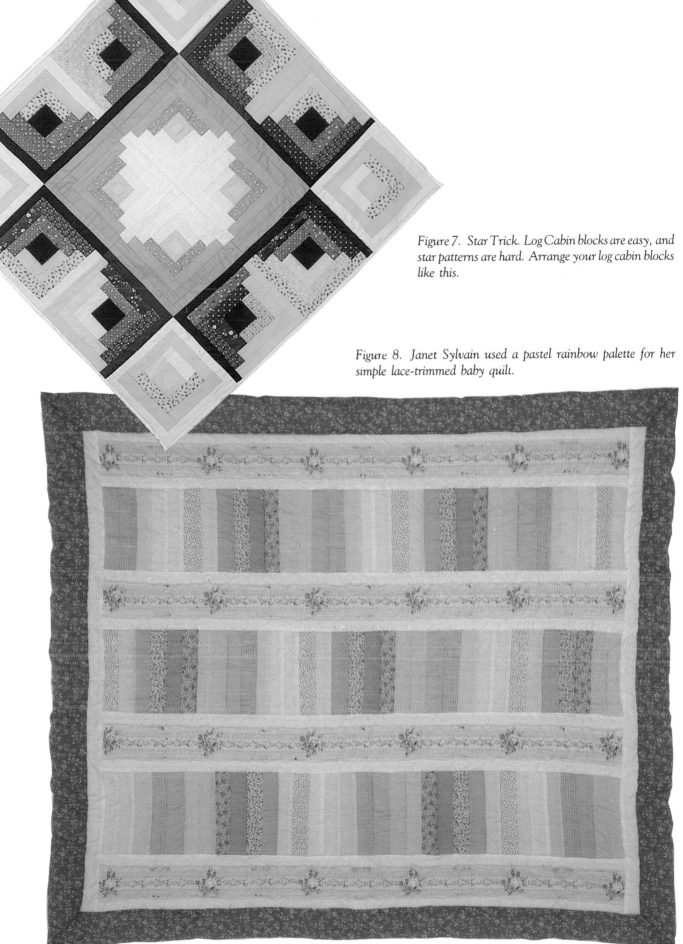

Figure 7. Star Trick. Log Cabin blocks are easy, and star patterns are hard. Arrange your log cabin blocks like this.

Figure 8. Janet Sylvain used a pastel rainbow palette for her simple lace-trimmed baby quilt.

Figure 9. *Just some strip-pieced panels and some bubble gum pink, but this Chinese Coins quilt by Gwen Marston and Joe Cunningham is a jewel.*

Figure 10. *"Too Much Fun" (opposite page) by Annie Taylor, is a riot of color. It reminds me of the improvisational freedom seen in Afro-American quilts. Surrounding the quilt is the backing fabric: is this perfect, or what?*

Figure 11. Louise Townsend created "Tunnel of Love." It was assembled by machine, then accented with a bit of hand quilting. (Photograph by Jerry DeFelice, courtesy of Quilter's Newsletter Magazine.)

CHAPTER TWO

TOOLS YOU'LL USE— AND WHAT YOU CAN DO WITHOUT

Go to a quilt show and you'll come away believing that you have to spend hundreds of dollars and add a room to your house in order to make a quilt. And it *is* fun to splurge on new tools and machines. But it isn't necessary. You can probably start with what you already have. What do we really, *really* need to make a quilt?

Sewing Machine

You *can* get by without a sewing machine, I understand, but I have no personal knowledge of this. I think you really need a sewing machine to produce a good strong quilt. It's exciting to have a new, top-of-the-line machine that will write your name and wake you up in the morning, but a fancy machine is not at all necessary. You need, most of all, a friendly machine. If yours is grouchy, clean it and oil it and give it a new needle. That cheers most of them up adequately. If yours is still stubborn, take it in for a professional tune-up. Some of the techniques we'll talk about require a zigzag-stitch machine, but there are ways to skirt around that requirement if your machine makes only a straight stitch.

Serger

A couple of the quilts in this book were made, all or in part, with a serger. Sergers are splendid little machines that can sew far faster than a conventional sewing machine while simultaneously trimming and overcasting the seam edge. They're great fun but are not necessary for a quiltmaker. If you have one, though, you might as well use it for

Figure 2-1. Sergers are fast and fun, but they're not absolutely necessary in quiltmaking. (Photograph by author.)

quilts as well as for the tee-shirts so often associated with the serger.

Scissors

You *must* have either good, sharp shears or a rotary cutter and mat (see next item). Ideally, you'll have both. You also need some smaller scissors to snip threads at the sewing machine. If you're going to cut paper patterns, get some inexpensive shears just for paper, cardboard templates, etc.

Rotary Cutter and Mat

The rotary cutter is a serious little tool that looks somewhat like a pizza cutter with a much smaller cutting blade. (They come in two sizes.) Using the cutter, you'll be able to slice through six layers of fabric with speed and accuracy. In early 1990,

they cost around $10; blades are replaceable when they become dull. Use a special self-healing mat with your cutter; it's absolutely necessary. Get the largest one you can afford. I like the mats that are marked off in 1″ grids. Rotary cutters and mats revolutionized quiltmaking when they appeared on the sewing scene. Mary Ellen Hopkins calls rotary cutters "whizzy whackers," and you can, too, in the privacy of your own home. Just don't ask for a whizzy whacker when you go to the fabric store.

Pins

Use good-sized pins with big glass or plastic heads. They're easier to pick up than smaller pins, and the big heads make them harder to lose in quilts—ouch! You should not sew over pins with your sewing machine for several reasons, including safety. If a pin gets bent or otherwise bollixed,

throw it away. A burred or bent pin makes for grouchy sewing. In addition to straight pins, you'll find safety pins useful for pin-basting. For many quilts, you can substitute safety-pinning for basting with long hand stitches. That's going to save you some time. (You can pin-baste with straight pins, but they tend to slip and get lost.) Choose nonrusting safety pins in a medium size.

Templates

Once *de rigueur*, templates are now optional. The rotary cutter has made some of them obsolete. I still use them, because I sew so much with scraps. If you're cutting 20 squares from new yardage, all you need is a whack or two with the rotary cutter and a good ruler, and you're done. No template needed.

If, however, you need 20 squares from 12 wildly irregular bits of scrap fabric, the easiest way to cut them is to lay down a plastic or metal template, trace around it, and cut it out with your scissors. There are some great clear plastic templates on the market that enable you to see ex-

actly what your square of fabric will look like. This way you can center that rose or lamb perfectly on every square. I have made and used cardboard templates in the past but have learned to be cautious. After you've marked around a cardboard template 10 or 20 times, its edges are worn. The fifteenth diamond is not the same shape as the first.

You can cut your own plastic templates from several brands of plastic sheets. Aleene's produces a plastic sheet you can use for cutting templates or for shrink art. Cutting a plastic template is as easy as cutting a cardboard template, but it carries the decided advantage of stability. Your fifteenth diamond cut from a plastic template, either a purchased one or one you've custom made, *will* be exactly the same as your first.

Needles

Like thread, needles are tiny, inexpensive, and often overlooked, yet they are vitally important. Sewing-machine needles come in varying thicknesses, and you should match them to the thick-

Figure 2-2. Templates come in lots of shapes and sizes. Some are clear, allowing for precise choosing of the design or motif to be cut.

ness of the fabric you're using. A size 12 or 14 (European size 80 or 90) needle will suffice for most medium-weight woven fabrics, and that's probably what you'll be using at first. Use a size 10 (70) needle for batiste, lightweight cotton, and silk; use a size 16 (European 100) needle for denim or similar heavy fabrics. Needle sizes range from 8/9 (65) for very sheer fabrics to 18 (110) for the heaviest denims.

I generally buy what is called a universal needle. It has a modified ball point for use on wovens as well as knits. Though I seldom sew with knits, the universal needle saves me the hassle of ferreting out a needle with a ball point when those rare occasions arise.

After you finish a quilt, throw your sewing-machine needle away and put in a new one.

For bindings and the occasional hand stitch, pick up a packet of hand-sewing needles in assorted sizes. For tying quilts you'll need a big strong needle with an eye large enough to accommodate yarn or whatever you're tying with.

Presser Feet

Use your regular foot for straight stitching. Your machine may or may not have another foot for zigzag stitching. Some machines have special embroidery feet for working satin-stitch embroidery. This foot is cut out underneath so it can pass over the stitches that build up without catching on them. A darning foot is ideal for free-motion machine quilting. You can see right where you're stitching, and the foot holds the fabric in place just loosely enough to allow it to move freely under the needle. A walking foot, or even-feed foot, is useful for straight-line machine quilting. Such a foot keeps all the layers traveling at the same pace so that the backing doesn't bunch up and wrinkle.

Acquire specialized presser feet only as they become necessary. You can make hundreds of good quilts with the few feet that came with your machine.

Markers

In addition to a common pencil, have within easy reach a water-erasable (wash-out) marker and an air-erasable (fade-away) marker. The former looks like a blue felt-tip. It glides easily across fabric, causing no pulling or distortion of the weave. Use it to mark quilting lines or appliqué placement or whatever you like. If you wash the piece after completing it, the lines will disappear. If you don't need to wash your quilt, just dab the lines with a wet paper towel or spray them with a mister; the marks will disappear instantly. Most air-erasable markers look like purple felt-tips. Depending upon temperature and humidity, marks made with these fade away within 12 to 48 hours.

You may need to make marks on dark fabrics from time to time. There are white chalk markers on the market for this very purpose, but I like to use a white Berol Prismacolor pencil. These are available in art-supply stores and cost less than a dollar. Besides, I love these pencils on general principle and have a full set of them handy for quilt designing and other art projects.

Iron

You need an iron to press seams. You'll be happier with a steam iron, but you can get by with just a dry iron. An iron that turns itself off can be a real nuisance to quilters. A person ironing the family laundry (who does that anymore, anyway?) who walks away for an hour has probably made a serious error in reasoning; a quilter is busy and mindful and wants the iron to be ready when she is. An ironing-board cover marked off in 1″ grids is a marvelous boon to quilters and regular stitchers alike. It's helpful in cutting, trimming, and pressing.

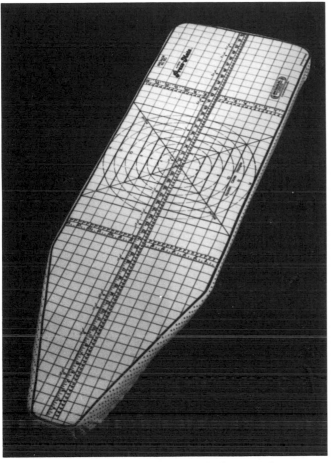

Quilt Frames

I bought a nice wooden freestanding quilt frame at a yard sale for $5. The woman who sold it had signed up for a quilting class, bought the frame, and never used it. This says a lot about her first quilting class, but it also speaks volumes about buying too much too soon. If you choose hand quilting over machine quilting, you can quilt without any frame at all, you can quilt in a large embroidery hoop, you can quilt in a small wooden lap frame, or you can quilt in a snap-apart PVC frame. After you've made several quilts, determine whether you want to make more and improve your hand-quilting technique; *then* think about a "real" quilting frame.

Figure 2-3. An ironing board cover marked off in inch squares is a big help in quiltmaking. (Photograph courtesy of June Tailor.)

CHAPTER THREE
SOFTWARE—FABRIC, BATTING, AND THREAD

Fabric

Have you seen Justin Wilson, the Cajun cook and comedian, on television? After telling you how to prepare some Louisiana delicacy, he goes on to tell you what kind of wine to drink with it, and it's always the same: "any kind you like." Well, that's pretty much the story on fabric, too, up to a point. Oh, it's true that many traditional quilters won't touch anything that's not 100% cotton, and there *are* occasions when you really need it. Don't even think about learning to hand appliqué, for instance, with anything else. Fabric that is 100% cotton is easy to work with, feels good, looks good, and wears well. It's fine stuff, and if you're going for the hand-pieced, hand-quilted masterpiece, you'd better seek it out and use it.

Cotton also has some other benefits. Fabric that is 100% cotton is more forgiving than the same weight and weave of cotton fabric with even 20% polyester mixed in. So if you're easing a binding around a corner, teasing a difficult pointed patch into a star, or hand appliquéing a dogwood blossom onto a field of stems and leaves, you definitely want cotton. Cotton feels better to the touch than does a cotton-poly blend, it takes dye a little differently, and it breathes (although with a layer of polyester batting behind it, this attribute loses its significance).

Then there's bearding. Bearding is the tendency for the batting fibers to work their way out through the quilt fabric, giving the effect of an old man's beard—hence the name. Most of the bat-

ting on the market today, at least the batting that's commercially available without going through mail order, is polyester, and it's easier for polyester fibers in the batting to migrate through polyester fibers in the quilt fabric than it would be for them to travel through a natural fiber. So cotton is superior from this aspect, too.

However, if the big rose print of your dreams is 65% polyester and 35% cotton, go for it. Polyester is harder to hand quilt than is an all-cotton fabric, but if you're tying or machine quilting, that fact shouldn't hold you back. I like rayon, but it creeps and slides and stretches. You can safely add some rayon strips to a Log Cabin quilt or any of the designs pieced to a foundation fabric, but don't use it for a main ingredient until you're fairly accomplished in maneuvering fabrics.

In fact, it's a good rule to choose the quilt you want to make first—and then consider fabric specifications. Now I wouldn't use 100% polyester for the cat to have kittens on, much less for a quilt, but that's my personal problem. I have seen some art quilts that incorporate polyester fabrics successfully. But for our baby quilts, let's avoid all-polyester fabric for now.

The only silk I'd recommend to the beginner is a matte-finish, medium-weight weave called silk noil. It's as easy to work with as an all-cotton broadcloth and takes dye beautifully. Colors really sing in silk. Now, lest you think I've taken leave of my senses, let me assure you about a couple of things. I hesitate to interject unpleasantries like spit-up and worse into this artistic discussion, but this is still the real world. Babies are apt to let go with fluids, solids, and varied mixtures. We know that. Silk noil is *almost* as tough and washable as a good cotton broadcloth. It's not an irrevocable disaster if little Jason reverses the digestive process on his quilt. The second factor you might question is price. Silk is fabulously expensive, isn't it? Some is, all right, but silk noil compares with (again) good cotton broadcloth when it comes to paying for it.

Check Chapter 14 for details about other fabrics you might want to use, such as corduroy, velveteen, and metallics. And if you want to learn more, look into Claire Shaeffer's absolutely definitive *Fabric Sewing Guide*. It's in the Book List at the back of this book.

How about mystery fabrics? If your cousin gives you her scrap bag, or if you take my advice and shop for fabric at the Goodwill, you'll come up with mystery fabrics. Just use your good sense. Compare the fabric with an all-cotton fabric, then with a cotton blend. Polyester fabrics feel slightly greasy to the touch, while natural fibers have a harder or crunchier feeling. Snip off a sample and burn it: Natural fibers leave a soft grey ash, while synthetics leave a hard, usually black, ball of residue.

Speaking of burning, how about the cotton-flannel scare? You know, those labels that say, "Warning. Not for use in children's sleepwear." Are you endangering the child's safety by incorporating a cotton-flannel square or strip here and there? Or by using it for interlining or even backing? Not at all. Obviously, almost any fabric is going to be flammable, so you don't really need to use extra care when it comes to cotton flannel.

True, untreated cotton or rayon will burn more quickly than will some types of nylon or polyester, while brushed, textured fabrics (like flannel) will burn more quickly than will tight weaves (like percale or broadcloth). But since there isn't that much difference in burning time, use whatever you want.

I'd advise you not to use loosely woven fabrics or fabrics you think will fade.

Whether you play it safe with all-cotton prints or strike out boldly with corduroy, velveteen, or denim, prewash your fabrics as soon as you get them home so you won't have to delay your creative genius when you're ready to make something beautiful.

Batting

Most quilts have a layer of batting sandwiched between the top and the backing, although some of the quilts in this book don't use batting. I've made many fine quilts substituting old blankets for batting. If you choose to use a blanket inside your quilt, you'll want to run it through the washer and dryer first.

There are battings available in cotton and wool, and even in silk, but you'll mostly find polyester batting in the stores. It's fluffy, washable, and durable, and thus quite satisfactory. Fairfield's battings include a needlepunched polyester that needs no more quilting than a blanket, high- and low-loft polyester and a 20% polyester–80% cotton blend. Most of the batting companies produce similar products. A new arrival on the batting scene is Warm & Natural's needlepunched unbleached cotton. It is lovely stuff. Another new product is the first dark batting available, called Polydown-DK (made by Hobbs Bonded Fibers). If you use Polydown-DK when making a dark-colored quilt, bearding won't be nearly as noticeable as it would be if you were to use regular light-colored batting. The many different batting lofts and materials available make it

easy to get just the effect you want for your quilt.

You'll find batting without too much trouble; it's in discount department stores and the like. You can also order it from many of the catalogs listed in Sources of Supply at the back of this book.

Thread

Thread is cheap; buy the best. If you're tempted by bargain bins of Brand X thread, walk on by. Thread is of prime importance; it has to hold all those little pieces together, and you don't want it to break or wear out. Cheap thread can also contribute mightily to a grouchy sewing experience, as it breaks, snarls, curls up in your bobbin case, and won't come out. Use all-cotton, polyester, or

Figure 3-1. Start with high-quality all-purpose sewing thread; you'll enjoy adding specialty threads to your collection as you go along.

cotton-wrapped polyester thread in your machine. Metrosene and Coats Dual Duty are two reliable brands, and there are several others.

You can add specialty threads to your collection as you go. Shiny rayons are great for machine embroidery and in the loopers of your serger, but they're not strong enough to hold the quilt pieces together. Quilting thread is heavier than regular sewing thread and is easier to use when you're hand quilting. In a pinch, there's no reason you can't quilt by hand with regular sewing thread. You can machine quilt with almost everything that'll go through the needle. Many quilters use metallic threads for extra glitter and sparkle; however, some of us find that they break frequently, lessening our quilting enjoyment.

CHAPTER FOUR
PUTTING IT ALL TOGETHER

There are lots of good books available on quilt-making technique. In the Book List, you'll find several excellent ones. Bonnie Leman and Louise Townsend's *How to Make a Quilt* captures everything you need to know between its paperback covers. Diana McClun and Laura Nowne's *Quilts! Quilts!! Quilts!!!* contains a good beginner's course, along with more advanced techniques, color theory, and specific patterns. Since I've already confessed to a slapdash approach, it would be redundant, if not downright silly, for me to tell you the right way to put your quilt together. Here, though, are the basic rudiments you'll need to complete the quilts in this book.

All the piecing directions are given with the individual quilts. All piecing is done by machine, usually with a $\frac{1}{4}''$ seam allowance and usually with the right sides of the fabric facing one another.

Pressing

In general, it's a rule that we press a seam before we cross it with another seam. There the agreement ends. Some stitchers swear that seams must be pressed to one side for strength. If you do press your seams to one side, press them toward the darker fabric to avoid a shadow. Other stitchers say that's nonsense, that our sturdy, machine-pieced seams may just as well be pressed open. I've gone through phases of using both pressing methods, and the quilts done both ways are still holding together. So press your seams whichever way works best for your fabrics and design.

Borders

You can add borders to most of these quilt designs. Directions for "Opti-Dots" in Chapter 8 tell how to do straight, unmitered borders. There's not much to it. If you get tired of sewing squares or strips together, just stop and add some borders. You'll know whether to do this or not by the way the quilt looks. For example, look at "Butterfly Squiggles" in the color section (Figure 18). Borders would be all wrong. They'd hold the butterflies in, confine them. The narrow white binding is all that design could use.

Making the Sandwich

Although some quilts have no batting and some use an interlining (like cotton flannel or muslin), most quilts are composed of three layers: the top, a layer of batting, and the backing fabric. If you use a blanket inside rather than batting, the sandwiching technique is still the same.

After washing, drying, and pressing the backing fabric, lay it right side down on a flat surface. Some quilters like to use masking tape to hold the fabric securely to the table, floor, or whatever the flat surface is. I don't find that necessary.

Lay the batting (or blanket) smoothly on the backing. Lay the quilt top, right side up, on top of the batting.

Starting from the center, safety-pin the layers together. You can also baste them together using a contrasting color thread and taking long, loose stitches. Most quilt directions advise basting in straight lines radiating out from the center, but that's not absolutely required. Do what's easy for you.

Quilting

Hand quilting is more beautiful, even when done by a beginner, than machine quilting or tying. With today's bonded and needle-punched battings, you can get by with very little quilting, so you might want to try hand quilting. I told myself for years I wouldn't do it, but much to my surprise, I find I enjoy hand quilting enormously. The basic premise is a simple running stitch; the trick is to make these stitches tiny and even. Don't worry about that—it'll happen in time, and even on your first quilts the baby won't examine your stitches.

Another trick to work on is hiding the thread knots. What you do: Tie a knot in the end of your thread and pull it through the sandwich from the back. Pull it just until it pops through the backing fabric. This buries the knot inside the quilt, and you're ready to stitch. To finish, you do basically the same thing, tying the knot on the top side of the quilt, then pulling it through just until it pops through the top and bringing the needle out an inch or so from the last stitch.

Machine quilting is fast, easy, and very durable. It can also be quite attractive. You can use a colorless nylon thread on top that will blend in with all your colors. You may find that it's hard to keep the layers of the sandwich together as you

stitch; if that happens, you might want to buy a walking foot (also called an even-feed foot) to control that problem. Until I machine quilted a corduroy coverlet, I never needed one. Again, you'll have to experiment. See the Book List for a very comprehensive book on the subject.

Tying a quilt is quickest of all, and it results in a puffy, cloudlike comforter. Use yarn, embroidery floss, narrow ribbon, or crochet cotton threaded through a crewel or other large-eyed needle. Use bonded or needle-punched polyester batting so that it will stay together with use. Come up on one side, leading a 3″ tail. Take a big stitch back down through all the layers and tie the resulting tail to the first tail in a square knot. The ties can be either on the top or on the back side of the quilt. You might need help in pulling the needle through all the layers. A leather thimble would help here; or you can use a deflated balloon to help grasp and pull. There's also a streamlined knot-tying technique explained in the directions for "Check It Out" in Chapter 14.

You can combine tying and machine quilting by machine tying your quilt. Begin with stitch width and length at 0. Hold the thread ends and stitch in one place two to three times to lock stitches. Set stitch width as wide as it'll go. Make 5 or 6 stitches, one on top of the other, through all layers of the quilt sandwich. This is basically a bar tack. Then set stitch width to 0 again and lock stitches. You can also stitch across a length of

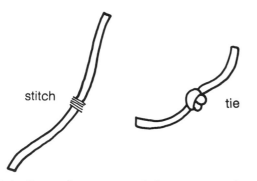

stitch   tie

Figure 4-1. For machine tying, stitch the yarn to attach it to the quilt, and then tie a knot right over the stitching.

yarn, then tie the yarn ends over the machine stitching. This method, shown in Figure 4–1, results in what looks like a hand-tied knot going through all layers.

Binding

Binding a quilt is not an exciting process, but because it means you're finished, it is actually a real thrill to cover up those last raw edges.

You can cut your binding strips on the straight grain of the fabric or on the bias. Obviously you'll use a lot less fabric if it's cut straight. It's harder to ease a straight-grain strip around the corners, but there are ways to circumvent that difficulty—such as not easing around the corners at all, but rather ending each strip at the corner.

I like to use satin for quilt binding. It adds a dressy shine, and it feels good to the touch. Babies especially enjoy a satin binding. However, satin is not a tough fabric, and a satin binding will wear out long before the rest of the quilt. Luckily, rebinding a quilt is a quick and easy task. When giving a quilt as a gift, I offer to put a new binding on when the original binding wears out. If you don't tell the new parents that you know the satin binding will wear out soon, they may be embarrassed and not know what to do about it. To me, the tactile and visual luxury of a satin binding is worth doing the job over every two or three years.

Ultrasuede makes a marvelous binding. It feels good and lasts forever. In addition, there are no edges to turn under, and the whole process can be done on the sewing machine. Drawbacks: It's pricey and comes in limited colors. I use my scraps. It takes a little longer, but all you have to do is overlap a new strip when you come to the end of an old one. No piecing is necessary, because Ultrasuede doesn't ravel. If you decide to bind your quilt with this miracle synthetic, follow the instructions in the paragraph below.

Cut Ultrasuede 1″ wide. Beginning at a corner, stitch wrong side of binding to backing side of quilt about ¼″ from quilt edge. Sew at very edge

of binding. Sew binding to one side of quilt and trim even with corner. Turn binding to right side and machine stitch, again right near the edge of the Ultrasuede. Go on to the next side. Corners are easy because you don't need to turn under any edges.

If you're using satin or another medium-weight woven fabric, cut your strips $1\frac{1}{2}''$ to $2''$ wide. Press the strip in half lengthwise, wrong sides facing. Stitch the cut edges to the right side of quilt top about $\frac{1}{4}''$ from edge. This gives you a neat, easy fold to bring over the seam and hand stitch to the backing fabric. This double, or French, binding also lasts longer than a regular binding.

A single, or regular, binding is cut in strips about $1\frac{1}{2}''$ wide. Machine stitch the right side of the binding to the right side of the quilt top. Fold binding over to the back of the quilt, turn the raw edge under, and hand stitch to the backing fabric.

One method used to get around the corners is to begin and end binding at the corners. Machine stitch binding (double or single) to opposite sides of quilt as directed. Turn to back and hand sew to backing fabric. Now machine stitch binding to the two remaining sides, leaving $\frac{1}{2}''$ ex-

tensions on both ends. Turn those extensions under, then turn binding to the back and finish stitching the binding down. Although straight machine stitching is shown for clarity in Figure 4–3, stitching the binding to the backing fabric is usually done by hand.

You can also miter the binding at the corners. Sew together enough binding strips to go around the quilt. Beginning along one edge, sew binding (double or single) to the right side of quilt top. When you are $\frac{1}{4}''$ from the corner, backstitch and take the needle out of the fabric. Fold up some extra fabric and turn the quilt to get ready to stitch the next side. Backstitch to begin, and

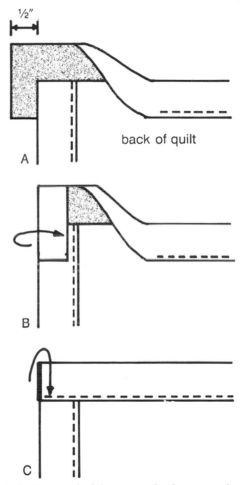

Figure 4-3. One method for sewing binding around corners. A. Leave extension on opposite ends of quilt. B. Fold extension under. C. Finish hand-sewing binding.

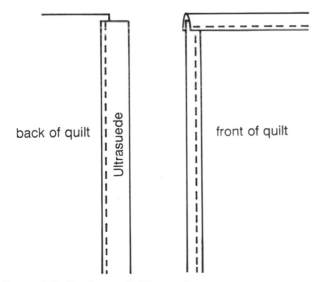

Figure 4-2. Binding with Ultrasuede.

finish sewing binding along that side. When you've machine stitched binding to all four sides of the quilt top, turn the binding over the seam to the backing fabric. Begin hand sewing to backing along one edge. When you reach the corner, fold the extra fabric neatly to ease it around the corner. You'll have to take a couple of extra stitches to hold the fold in place.

Some quilters like to trim the corners in a gentle curve before using any of these binding methods. Some quilts lend themselves to rounding the corners; some don't.

There's yet another easy way to bind a quilt. Cut your backing fabric a couple of inches larger

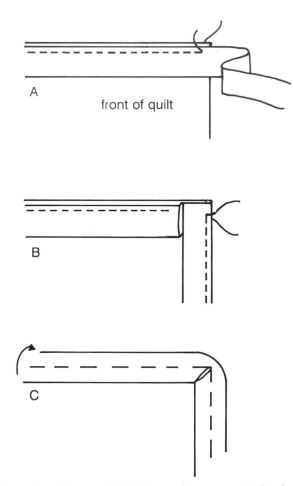

Figure 4-4. Mitering the binding at the corners. A. Stitch to $\frac{1}{4}$" from corner, break stitching. B. Fold up extra fabric, sew next side of binding. C. Turn binding over to back of quilt; hand stitch in place.

than your quilt top. Fold the excess backing over to the front, fold the raw edges under, and hand stitch the fold to the front of the quilt. You can either miter the corners or not. I've seen quilts, too, with the front folded over to the back. It's uncommon, but you can do it.

Signing

Lots of quilt directions end with the instruction, "Sign and date your quilt." I think this is very important, but for me, it's too late. I don't hand embroider very well, and what other way is left to sign and date a finished quilt? You should take care of this step earlier in the game. Do it at the earliest, most effective place in the process. You can use free-motion machine embroidery on the quilt top or on the backing fabric, sign it with a permanent marker, or make a little pocket to sew onto the backing fabric. Into that pocket, you can tuck a note with more historical information than you'd want to write or stitch onto the quilt itself. You can also type on a nonwoven interfacing or spray-starched woven fabric, then sew that to the backing. Another advantage to signing the quilt early, before it's finished, is that you aren't so tempted to judge your work. You know: "I'd sign this quilt, but it's not good enough" and that sort of thing. Sign and date them all. You don't have to decide whether or not you're proud of your quilt. You're just a reporter on her beat, a historian at her desk. (I say this. Do I do this? No, but I plan to start right away.)

Laundering, or Cats and Cigarettes

Complete directions for washing and drying our nonmuseum-quality quilts are given in Chapter 18, "Caring for Your Quilt." The topic to be considered here is whether to do so or not. If you've taken the most rudimentary care while making your quilt, and if you haven't bled on it or

spilled your coffee on it, you probably don't need to wash it before presenting it to the new baby. (Or the five-year-old child—I know how long one can procrastinate.)

However, if you smoke, or if any of your housemates smoke, your quilt is going to smell like cigarettes. Even worse, it's going to smell like stale cigarettes. You probably won't notice this, but people who don't smoke *will*. And the new baby will. In this case, you won't have to do a major cleaning job on the finished quilt, but you really should suds it out very lightly, rinse it thoroughly, and dry it carefully just before presentation. If you keep it around several days or weeks, that cigarette scent will creep right back into the fibers. If you don't want to wash the quilt, air it by hanging it outside, out of direct sun, for an hour or two. On this subject I'm being pragmatic, not preachy. I used to smoke, and I had to wash all my baby quilts when I finished them, too.

Now, on to cats. I have fed and sheltered cats since I was a kid, and every cat I've known has shown a fierce interest in projects in progress. "Ah," they seem to say, "you're working on another one. Let's give it the old grooming-and-nap test." Now, unless Puff had muddy paws or the like, it depends on the recipient whether or not you need to launder the finished piece. If the child is healthy, several months old, and you can shake or brush the visible hair off, I'd probably advise you not to bother washing the quilt. You most likely know the Scotch-tape trick if you're a cat-keeper. You probably use it on all your black skirts. For those who are not familiar with this trick: Just make a tape loop and dab it all over the quilt, replenishing the tape as it becomes too fuzzy to work. If you're giving the quilt to a family that also houses cats, I certainly wouldn't recommend that you bother with more than a cursory tape-cleaning. If the baby is newborn or is known to have allergies or other sensitivities, you'd better launder the quilt lightly before presentation.

CHAPTER FIVE

CHEATING AND OTHER TECHNIQUES

We'll discuss ways to squeeze, stretch, improvise, and otherwise fudge (without harming the quilt in any way) in the directions for the specific quilts. What we'll say there, in a nutshell, is not to compromise the structural integrity of the quilt. You know: Don't use cheap fabric that will fall apart; don't take such a narrow seam that it will come unstitched; that sort of thing.

Let's talk here about some of the conflicts that arise between the art of making a quilt—or anything else that's important to you, from a chocolate soufflé to a water-lily pond—and the current emphasis on women's self-esteem. (As much as I'd like to believe that half you readers are men, it's not true, and I know it. So let's talk for a minute woman-to-woman.)

You deserve a good work space, good tools and good materials, and free time to play and create without worrying about making dinner. I think we all agree on that. You are the one who must claim these things, go out and get them, and preserve your right and freedom to use them. Neither your husband, your children, your mother, or society at large will insist that you have these things. If you don't sell your work, you may have to justify spending money on your own pleasure—to others or to yourself. Take it from me—even write it on your wall—you deserve it.

Now let's look at the flip side of this situation. You have the privilege of balancing this "serious" aspect of your quiltmaking with the "fun" part of creating. For example: It's almost midnight, and you're rolling right along on your quilt. You've cut out 60 blue squares from $4-per-yard 100% cotton broadcloth for your Trip

Around the World baby quilt. All your other squares lie there in neat stacks. Suddenly you realize that you need 20 more blue squares, and you're out of that particular fabric. Now, do you put your quilt away and wait until the fabric store opens in the morning? Or do you cut your additional squares from some blue cotton-polyester print that picks up the hot pink of the next row of squares?

The right answer is—either one. Whatever your little heart desires is all right. Now, if you're going to enter this quilt in a big regional show, if it's a star turn for you, you might want to wait. But if you choose that poly blend, it isn't because you're just "making do." It's because you want to get on with sewing squares together, you know you'll be able to arrange those squares so they'll look great, the baby will love it even more for its variations, and using that print might just make your quilt sing a whole new song. You *deserve* all-new, fine materials, but you also deserve your artistic freedom.

I advocate going to the Goodwill store to find fabric. It's often more inspirational than the fabric store. The fact that you'll pay less money at the Goodwill is only important if you're afraid of cutting into expensive fabric because you're afraid of messing up. The important fact is that you might find a batik skirt that you can cut into squares, juxtapose with muslin, and create a bright new unthought-of masterpiece quilt. Likewise, you have the freedom to rip out stitches and make a perfect match of seams, or the freedom to say, "That's how I want it. That's the way this quilt works."

Having read this far, you might accuse me of teaching sloppy technique. And I'd have trouble with my defense. However, I advocate casual quilting technique only to get you started. If you like the quilting process, you'll naturally improve

Figure 5-1. This improvisational strip quilt, made by an anonymous nineteenth-century quiltmaker, is pieced on both sides. (Photograph courtesy of the San Francisco Craft and Folk Art Museum, from Who'd A Thought It by Eli Leon.)

your technique. There are plenty of books and classes around to help you do that. (You may choose not to smooth out all the rough edges in your technique. Many "real" artists cherish and cultivate the spontaneous, the naïve.) But all the careful cutting and perfect piecing in the world won't make you love quilting. If you don't enjoy your first attempt, you may not—and probably won't—make a second try. Enjoyment is the prime ingredient in fashioning an active quilter. If you find pleasure in making a quilt, you're on your way, and my casual workmanship techniques shouldn't hold you back.

If you're still scared—if you still think that if your colors aren't perfectly coordinated and your little squares don't meet at the corners you're a doomed quilter—take a look at the Afro-American quilts that are enjoying such popularity today. These quilts are often so "off" that it's difficult to figure out how they were assembled. However, their energy and life jump right out and grab you.

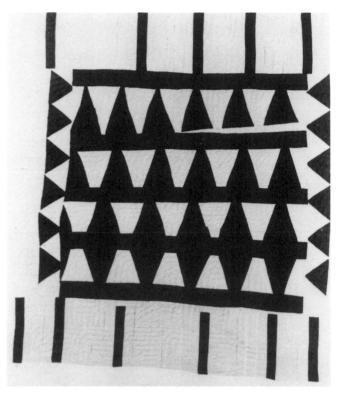

Figure 5-2. Another exuberant quilt in the African-American tradition: "Triangle Strip," pieced by Charles Cater and quilted by Willia Ette Graham. (Photograph courtesy of the San Francisco Craft and Folk Art Museum, from Who'd A Thought It by Eli Leon.)

CHAPTER SIX
SQUARE ROOTS

Literally hundreds of quilt designs can be made using squares only. In this section, we'll talk about some classic quilts that use one size square throughout, such as Trip Around the World, nine-patch, and charm quilts. We'll look at Irish chain quilts that are made from two sizes of squares, and we'll consider making quilts using cross-stitch or needlepoint charts. Some of these can be very effective using squares only, and some might need a triangle here and there.

Although I think cheating is very creative and that errors are divine opportunities for design development, I still have a stubborn, honest streak and cannot keep a secret. When I came across a photograph of Jean Ray Laury's "Lunar Madness" (see color section, Figure 2). I said, "Great, here's a perfect example of an art quilt that's subtle, flashy, easy, and tricky all at once. It's obviously made using only one size of square. Now if only Jean will let me show it in the book. . . ." Well, Jean readily agreed and sent me a picture of this great quilt. But she also informed me that it isn't a pieced quilt at all, but rather a silk-screen printed design. So, it was trickier than I'd guessed. Look at it, though. There is no reason you couldn't make a quilt like this with squares.

Below are two basic ways to cut squares, along with some hints for beginners. If you're making your first (or second or third) quilt, you'll probably want to start with squares at least 4″ in size. Cutting them smaller than that will slow you down quite a bit as a beginner; later on, you'll be cutting 2″ squares that'll stitch up into 1½″ eye-dazzling pointillist masterpieces. But for now, 4″ minimum. You'll see quilts that are not shabby at

all made from much larger squares. "Domenic's Quilt," shown in Figure 3 in the color section, is made from 8″ squares.

Cutting Squares Using a Template

Cut squares with a template or with a rotary cutter and ruled mat. Whichever way you choose, you'll want to make sure that the threads in the fabric are lined up with one straight edge of the square. This is called *on grain,* and it's vitally important in clothing construction and almost as important in quiltmaking. There's more discussion about templates and rotary cutters in Chapter 2, "Tools You'll Use—And What You Can Do Without."

Lay template down on fabric, checking that it's on grain. It doesn't matter if you place the template on the right or wrong side of the fabric. Trace around it with a marker (wash-out or fade-away) or a soft lead pencil. Don't use anything that will smear or fade when you wash the quilt. You'll be cutting along the marked line, but there'll still be traces of the line remaining. You

wouldn't want to use a ballpoint pen, for instance, because of the ink residue. Don't use a pencil or pen that requires very firm pressure to make a mark, or you'll pull the fabric and distort it.

After marking, cut along the marked lines. You can lay the template right up against the previous mark, of course, so that one cut does double duty.

Rotary Cutter Method

Using a straightedge, cut 4″-wide strips as long as fabric will allow. Hold the rotary cutter right up against the straightedge, keep your fingers away from the blade, and cut away from yourself. Although the cutter will easily slice through multiple layers of fabric, it's a little tricky to fold the fabric perfectly straight. Experiment with this technique a little.

After you've cut the 4″-wide strips, stack several of them neatly, and slice them into 4″ segments. Presto! Perfect 4″ squares with no marking.

We'll talk about several quilts that you can

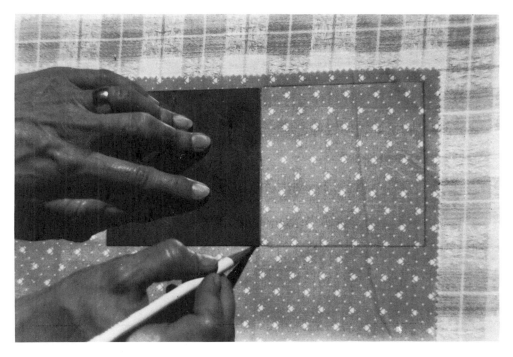

Figure 6-1. Templates are efficient when you're using scraps or when you want to isolate a motif.

use speed-cutting techniques with. In these, you'll assemble rows of strips, then cut them into already-pieced modules.

If you're working with scraps, the template method is easier; if you have new, uncut fabrics, you'll find the rotary-cutter method much faster.

It stands to reason that accuracy in cutting squares is important. It is, after all, the first step in the real nuts and bolts of the quiltmaking process (ignoring the mental work of designing, choosing fabric, etc.). Work carefully, but go have a cup of tea if you find yourself getting tense or compulsive about it.

After you've mastered quilts with one size of square, you can go on to quilts using several sizes of squares. A good book on this very subject is *Baker's Dozen Doubled,* which appears in the Book List at the end of this book.

Figure 6-2. Quilt design by Mary Ellen Hopkins, from Baker's Dozen Doubled.

CHAPTER SEVEN
TRIANGLE TRICKS

Many basic quilt blocks contain triangles. Triangles aren't all that difficult to work with; however, a consideration of the integral structure of woven fabric and its nature can help you to understand why they are inarguably trickier than squares, rectangles, and strips, which are all straight-grain pieces.

A woven fabric (and almost all of them *are* woven, except for felt, knits, and synthetic suedes) is composed of two sets of threads running at right angles to one another (one sets runs vertically, the other horizontally). Fabric stretches least along its length, or *warp.* It stretches a little bit more across its width, or *weft.* The most stretch of all occurs at a diagonal, or *bias.* No matter how carefully you handle the fabric in cutting, measuring, pinning, and stitching, bias cuts are going to stretch a little. If one quilt patch distorts just a tiny bit, there's not much problem. But if you're making a quilt composed of lots of triangles, that distortion multiplied 100 times can result in a quilt that, despite your best cheating techniques, just doesn't fit together at all.

We're going to explore some ways to achieve the diagonal look without fussing with bias cuts and seams. These methods will help you get started, and will prove valuable even when you're an accomplished quiltmaker.

Folded Square

You can place a square, folded to make a triangle, right over your basic square. This has the added benefit of making a little pocket, interesting for

baby's fingers and adult eyes alike. Cut two same-size squares instead of one, fold one in half diagonally, and press it cautiously with your iron or fingers. Lay it in place over the whole square and baste it along the edges. These steps are shown in Figures 7-1a and b. Now you can treat that multi-layer square as though it were a plain and unadorned square as you work it into your design.

Stitched and Folded Square

If you don't want the little pocket effect (cracker crumbs come immediately to mind as a good reason to exclude little pockets from baby quilts), or

if you'd like to vary your *faux* triangle look, you can stitch the fold down after you've placed your folded square on the whole square. The stretching on the bias will occur, but since you're sewing to a straight-grain piece, the integrity won't be compromised. Sew the fold down first, then baste to the base square, and you'll be able to trim away any stretched fabric before incorporating the square into the overall design.

Stitched Square

Sew a cut triangle to the base square with a double line of stitches along the raw edge of the triangle as shown in Figure 7-1c. Use a double needle in your machine if you have one, or just sew two lines of stitches. This cut edge will, of course, fray in time, but bias-cut edges don't fray as straight cuts do, and if this softened edge will work in the design you envision, there's no reason not to use it.

Prairie Points

Some quilts use prairie points for edging; some incorporate them into a seam. To make a prairie point, follow the folding method shown in Figure 7-2. Baste your folded and pressed prairie points to edges of a strip and sew the seam; you'll wind up with perky little triangles. Babies love the texture of these unexpected points. Use them in other ways, too; for instance, dinosaurs in "Dinosaur Parade" (Chapter 13) could have prairie points for those spikes down their backs.

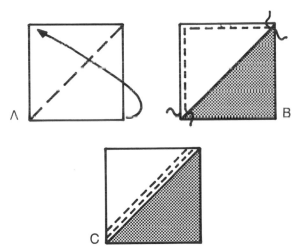

Figure 7-1. Folded square method for achieving the diagonal look. A. Fold one square diagonally and press carefully. B. Baste to two edges of second square to make a triangle. Or, C. Sew a cut triangle to a square with two lines of stitching.

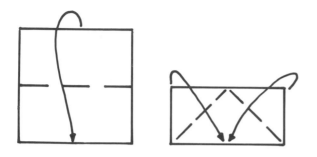

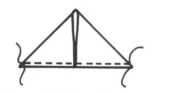

Figure 7-2. Folding method for making prairie points.

Rickrack

Add tiny, tiny triangles by tucking rickrack into a seam. I just saw a picture of a very funny quilt showing coyotes whose teeth were composed of white rickrack. (The quilt is by Carol Ann Wadley, and you can see it in the Summer 1989 issue of *American Quilter*, listed in the Publications List at the end of this book.)

Folded Geese

Flying geese is an old tradition quilt pattern, made by sewing three triangles together to form a rectangle, then adding more such units to make a strip of V's. (I have never been sure if each triangle is supposed to represent a single goose or the formation of the flock.) At any rate, here's a way to make flying geese with no triangles and no bias seams. This technique is similar to the hand-piecing technique of Afghani piecework (described in detail in *The Fabric Lover's Scrapbook;* see Sources of Supply at the end of this book).

Start with a strip of the base fabric, cut, let's say for learning purposes, 3″ wide. Cut several 3″ squares, some from an assortment of fabrics and some from one single fabric. The assortment will form the geese, while the main fabric makes up

the background. Fold all the squares in half with right sides out; press the fold. Lay a "goose" piece at the lower end of the base strip; stitch around all cut edges. Now lay 2 background pieces over it at angles, as shown in Figure 7-3. Follow with another goose, stitched around three sides leaving the fold free. Continue adding folded squares until your base strip is covered. Note that you'll

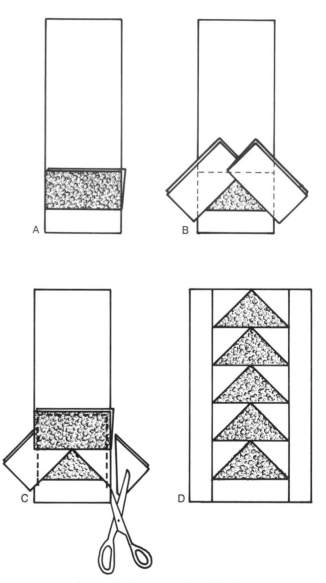

Figure 7-3. Making folded geese. A. Lay folded square on strip. B. Place two folded squares at angles. C. Add another folded square; stitch and trim. D. Finished strip, with strips sewn to sides.

have to trim off the extensions of the fabric beyond the base strip.

Drawn, Stitched, and Cut Triangles

These are also known as hassle-free triangles or PPT's (*perfectly pieced triangles*). The trick here is in sewing that pesky bias seam first. That leaves much less chance for stretching it out of shape. This method is good only for making sets of triangles that are to be preassembled into squares. In other words, it won't help you with your scrap triangles or with individual triangles that you don't plan to sew together into squares—but it is an excellent method for making two-triangle squares.

Like so many of the speed-cutting and speed-sewing methods quilters today take for granted, this innovative technique was developed by Barbara Johannah. Her *Quick Quiltmaking Handbook* was published in 1979 and was a real breakthrough.

Lay your two pieces of fabric out, right sides together, lighter color on top. Start with pieces no larger than 18″ × 22″. Decide on the finished size of your triangle and add on the seam allow-

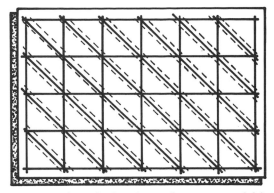

Figure 7-4. Stitch on broken lines, then cut on solid lines, to make easy two-color triangles.

ance. Now, according to the originator herself, the seam allowance is vital. Add $1\frac{3}{4}$″ and plan on using a $\frac{1}{2}$″ seam allowance.

Draw a grid on the top fabric—for instance, draw a 6″ grid. Now draw diagonal lines in one direction going through the corners (see Figure 7-4). Now stitch $\frac{1}{2}$″ on both sides of the diagonal lines you've drawn. Cut apart on all marked lines, vertical, horizontal, and diagonal. Presto! A set of two-color, $4\frac{1}{4}$″ squares formed from triangles.

(Why, you may be asking, use $\frac{1}{2}$″ seams? Because, says Barbara, the added seam allowance for $\frac{1}{4}$″ seams would be $\frac{7}{8}$″, and that's just too picky to work with.)

CHAPTER EIGHT

TRIP AROUND THE WORLD

This traditional quilt pattern gives a generous amount of drama for the effort. A one-patch design, it uses squares all of one size, arranged in a radiating diamond pattern. It's perfect for using up scraps, because each row of color doesn't have to be all the same fabric—and, in fact, it adds more interest if the fabrics almost match but don't quite. Here are general directions for making any Trip Around the World quilt.

General Directions

Cutting

See Chapter 6 for a description of the template method and the rotary cutter method. (If you're using scraps, use a template. If you're using fresh yardage, use a rotary cutter.) Cut more squares than you think you'll need. This makes arranging and rearranging more fun, and you'll always be able to use your leftovers. When I begin a Trip Around the World quilt, I usually don't know what color will go where. If you use only a few squares of one color near the center, you'll be able to use lots more of that same color when you're filling in the corners.

Arranging

You can use graph paper and colored pencils, but there's no substitute for actually laying the squares of fabric out on a flat surface (work outward from the center). Especially if you're using scrap fabrics and/or large prints, being able to move one square here and another one there can make a big difference. Squinting your eyes, looking at the arrangement in a mirror or through the

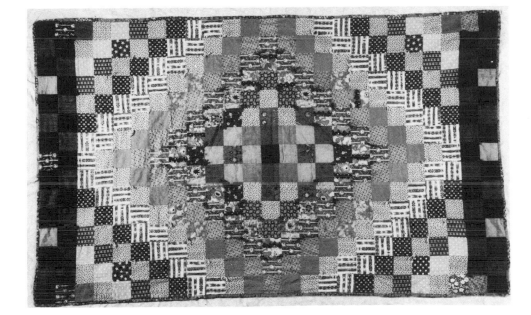

Figure 8-1. My son Evan's Trip Around the World quilt is over 10 years old. It has not had an easy life.

wrong end of binoculars, and taking a Polaroid photograph of the layout are valuable techniques for getting the overall impact of your design arrangement before you start sewing. You'll realize quickly that you need an uneven number of squares going across and down when you're making a Trip Around the World arrangement.

You can lay the squares out on a table, bed, or floor, but if you have a cardboard cutting board, you can more easily carry the final arrangement to your sewing machine.

Sewing

Pick up the squares from one row, horizontal or vertical, stacking one on top of the other. Place the stack of squares beside the sewing machine and sew them together. Set stitch length at about 14 stitches per inch; that's close enough to eliminate the need for backstitching, which can really slow you down. It doesn't matter how wide your seams are, as long as they're somewhere between $\frac{1}{4}''$ and $\frac{1}{2}''$ and are all the same width. Use your presser foot for a guide; they're all close enough to $\frac{1}{4}''$ for our purposes. As you finish each row, lay it down on the arrangement surface and pick up the next.

Pressing

Carry all your rows to the ironing area. Press the seams on the first row to the right, those on the second row to the left, and so on. Lift the iron as you move from place to place—don't slide it. This prevents stretching. Press lightly, just enough to flatten the seam out but not enough to

pull the fabric out of shape. You may or may not need steam, depending on your chosen fabrics. Lay the sewn rows back and make sure all squares are in the right arrangement.

Sewing Again

Pick up the first two rows. Pin them together at the most visible places. If you have solid colors mixed in with prints, for instance, pin at the solid color squares. The eye will see inaccuracies in a bright, solid, dark, or light area more easily than where four print squares join. When sewing the rows of "Trip to the Tropics" (see color section, Figure 4), for instance, I pinned at the solid turquoise squares.

Pick up the next 2 rows (rows 3 and 4) and sew them together. Sew rows in pairs, then join pairs to complete the quilt top.

Now, if your cutting and sewing were impeccable, every other seam will align perfectly. They probably won't, though. Put some cheating songs on the tape deck, and let's make this work.

Cheating

If your rows match up at the visually important places and vary slightly at the blending places, don't worry. Sew it together as is. If you need to, feel free to make little pleats at the corners, stretch squares slightly, or ease in fullness. Or, if two prints don't have much contrast between them, it's quite all right if the seams just don't match. What you *must not* do is sew a seam that's less than $\frac{1}{4}''$. That undermines the strength of the quilt, becomes the weak link, comes unstitched during the fifth washing, and so on.

Pressing Again

Press the quilt top (for the last time) from the back side, lifting the iron from place to place. Don't stretch the quilt.

Finishing

Finish according to the directions given in Chapter 4, "Putting It All Together."

Quilt 1:
Trip to the Tropics

Materials

Scraps or $\frac{1}{4}$-yard cuts of the following 45"-wide fabrics: solid-color turquoise, several blue-and-white tropical prints, red-and-white print, pink-and-white print; about 4 yards of backing fabric (this quilt is backed with muslin); one 4" square of solid-color hot pink; one purchased floral appliqué (optional); $\frac{1}{2}$ yard of blue chambray (or whatever) for binding; one 60" square of low-loft batting; sewing thread (I used grey throughout); white quilting thread

Tools

4" square template, rotary cutter and mat, sewing machine, quilting needle

Finished Size

60" square

Directions

1. Wash and dry all your fabrics; press if necessary.

2. Cut 289 4" squares from assorted fabrics. Stack by color.

3. Lay squares out on the floor, bed, cutting board, or another flat surface. Arrange in radiating diamonds in any order that pleases you.

4. Sew together in rows, then sew rows together, pressing after each phase of sewing. Press completed quilt top.

Figure 8-2. Quilt 1: "Trip to the Tropics."

5. If desired, sew floral appliqué in the center, stitching by hand or by machine. Mine is stitched by machine, using matching thread and a narrow zigag.

6. Complete the quilt, following directions in Chapter 4, "Putting It All Together." Cut blue chambray into 1½"-wide straight strips and bind quilt, beginning and ending each binding strip at the corners (explained in Chapter 4).

Notes: The only reason I added the floral appliqué was that, upon completing the quilt top, I decided that the center pink square was not vivid enough. The center square, or central area, of a Trip Around the World quilt should be strong, and this one wasn't. Sewing on the flower made it work fine. I call this explanation a "note" rather than "cheating," but I guess it is cheating, in a way. Had I been functioning absolutely per-

fectly, I'd have chosen a stronger color for that central square (which you may want to do for your quilt). The flower appliqué, however, resulted in an even stronger center. It is what it is.

I intended to take "Trip to the Tropics" to the ladies at the Sumner (Texas) Community Center to have it quilted. I had no intention of hand quilting this piece (or any other, at that time). But after finishing the quilt top, I realized that straight-line quilting would not show off the large tropical prints to full effect. They're the big story in this quilt. I put the quilt in my little Quick-Snap frame, took needle in hand, and quilted around the flower motifs every few rows. I did some straight-line quilting, too. When you use a good-quality bonded or needle-punched batting, you can get away with less quilting. This quilt will stand up to baby wear and tear.

Figure 8-3. Quilt 2: "Opti-Dots."

Quilt 2:
Opti-Dots

After I'd finished Trip to the Tropics, I decided it wasn't "typical" enough to use as my sole example of a Trip Around the World quilt. I thought I'd better make one with more solid colors. Well, Opti-Dots has more solid colors, all right, but it's still far from typical. Its solid colors vibrate intensely on their own, and the polka dot fabric only adds to the visual punch. Babies love bright colors, though, and it's certainly stimulating! (See color section, Figure 5.)

Materials

¼- to ¾-yard cuts of 45″-wide silk noil or cotton (see "Notes" at the end of the directions for this quilt) in red, hot pink, magenta (I used an old skirt), and teal blue; ½ yard of magenta and teal polka dot cotton; one 50″ square of low-loft batting; red sewing thread; red silk quilting thread; one 52″ square of red cotton broadcloth for backing; ¼ yard of 45″-wide lightweight red satin

Tools

Same as "Trip to the Tropics"; substitute a 3″ square template

Finished Size

50″ square

Directions

1. Wash and dry your fabrics; press if necessary.

2. Cut 225 three-inch squares from various fabrics, stack by color, and arrange to suit your fancy.

3. Sew squares together in rows, then sew rows together. Press.

4. Cut teal blue fabric into strips 3″ wide. Sew one strip to top, one to bottom of pieced squares; press. Sew teal strips to sides of quilt; press. (All these border-strip seams are also ¼″, more or less.)

5. Cut hot pink fabric into strips 2″ wide. Sew one strip to top, one to bottom of quilt. Sew hot pink strips to sides of quilt; press.

6. Cut red fabric into strips 3″ wide. Sew one strip to top, one to bottom of quilt. Sew red strips to sides of quilt; press.

7. Complete quilt, following directions in Chapter 4, "Putting It All Together."

8. Quilt by hand or machine. I laid masking tape across the quilt top diagonally and hand quilted along the tape. You can use one piece of tape three or four times before it loses its stickiness. Borders are quilted "in the ditch," which means quilting right in the seam line. Although you lose the effect of each individual stitch, it raises the entire area outlined.

9. Cut red satin into 1½″-wide strips. Piece strips together into a continuous length; then bind quilt, easing around corners. I rounded the corners of the quilt first to make it easier.

Notes: This quilt does have historical precedent. An inventory from Wales in 1551 lists "In the New Chamber over ye Garden . . . Item a quylte of redd sylke in the Nursery." (Quoted in "The newest quilt fad seems to be going like crazy" by Joseph Harriss, *Smithsonian,* May 1987.) I used silk noil only because I had it on hand. This quilt would be beautiful made with cottons or blends. And the silk quilting thread? I never intended that, either. When looking for red quilting ➡

thread, I found silk before I found cotton and then convinced myself that I deserved it. The quilt was first bound in red silk noil, but the fabric was so crunchy and had so much body that I could not negotiate the corners at ➡

all. This was a rare instance in which I took my seam ripper and tiny scissors in hand and undid the binding. Rationalizing didn't work. Motto: When in doubt, bind your quilt with red satin.

CHAPTER NINE

NINE-PATCH AND OTHER CLASSICS

In olden days, little girls were stitching up their first quilts when they were around five years old. One of the most popular patterns for these kiddie quilts was the basic nine-patch. You've seen a hundred of them, with and without sashing strips, some beautiful and some just utilitarian.

Figure 9-1. It's easy to center motifs perfectly if you use a see-through template.

First we'll discuss two ways to go about making the nine-patch block, and then we'll go on to a stunning example of the form, which I call "Nine from Gwen." Take a look at it in Figure 6 in the color section.

Nine-patch blocks are frequently separated by sashing strips or with big plain blocks alternating with the nine-patch blocks. Sometimes all the squares run together, and it's more difficult to see the nine-patch-ness of the design.

One way to make a nine-patch block, obviously, is to cut nine squares, sew them together in rows of threes, and then sew the rows together. This is the best way to set out if you're working with scrap fabrics. We've already talked about cutting and sewing squares (Chapters 6 and 8), so you know just about everything there is to know about this method. If you take a little extra time, work carefully, or use one of the see-through templates, you can center that lamb or that rose or whatever perfectly in each of your chosen squares. This is an easy way to dress up an otherwise plain quilt.

A speedier way to make two-color nine-patch blocks is to cut strips across the width of the two fabrics and then stitch the strips together in two different arrangements, as shown in Figure 9-2.

Cut these pieced strips into segments, re-stitch, and you've got your nine-patch block. When working with new yardage, this is definitely the way to go.

Figure 9-2. For speedy nine-patch blocks, sew strips like these, then cut and reassemble.

Quilt 3:
Nine from Gwen

When I called quilt teacher Gwen Marston to ask if we could use her "Chinese Coins" quilt in this book (see Chapter 11), she mentioned that she had a sweet little nine-patch as well, if I was interested. And of course I was. But I wasn't prepared for this spectacular quilt. No speed-stitching here; these scrappy little squares are dancing with diversity. Gwen, along with her partner, Joe Cunningham, has balanced the generous mixture of prints with muslin for a beautiful old-fashioned look. And the hand quilting,

which I'm not sure how well you'll be able to see in the photograph, is lavish. The border is filled with delicate stitches in a graceful, flowing feather motif set off with triangles. Now if I were going to do this *tour de force* hand quilting, I'd make sure it was worked on a contrasting solid-color fabric so nobody would miss my efforts. Not Gwen and Joe. This fabulous quilting is just casually flung down onto a field of tiny flowers. Ah, well.

You are probably not going to cut 819 little squares measuring 1½″, but these directions can be easily adapted to make a nine-patch quilt with larger blocks and simpler setting. But what do I know? You might decide to duplicate this quilt and succeed admirably. So here goes.

Materials

45″-wide cotton fabrics as follows: 1½ yards of tiny red print, 1 yard of solid-color gold, ½ yard of muslin, lots of scraps of print fabrics, 2 yards of backing fabric (this quilt is backed with red and yellow paisley); a 46″ × 70″ piece of low-loft quilt batting; sewing thread; white quilting thread

Tools

Template for 1½″ square (optional), sewing machine, scissors or rotary cutter and mat, quilting needle (optional)

Finished Size

46″ × 70″

Directions

1. Wash and dry fabrics; press if necessary.

2. Assemble nine-patch blocks by either method. This quilt contains 91 nine-patch blocks; each block measures 3″ when completed and stitched. All seams are the standard ¼″.

3. This quilt is bound with solid-color gold bias

Figure 9-3. "Nine from Gwen." (Photograph by author.)

Figure 9-4. The borders of "Nine from Gwen" are hand quilted with this feather motif.

strips. If you're going to do the same, go ahead and cut your strips. You'll need about 240″ of 1¼″-wide bias strips. Seam strips together to make a continuous length; set aside.

4. From remaining gold fabric, cut ninety-six 2″ squares. From red print, cut 188 rectangles measuring 2″ × 3½″.

5. Sew a red rectangle to each side of 7 nine-patch blocks to make the first row. Strip will look like Figure 9-5. Repeat to make 13 such rows. This will use up all your nine-patch blocks.

6. Sew 13 red rectangles to sides of 12 gold squares to make a row that looks like Figure 9-5. Repeat to make 12 such rows.

7. Sew a row of nine-patch/red rectangles to a row of gold square/red rectangles. Sew another row, stitching rows together in pairs and then assembling pairs until quilt top is completed. Press top.

8. From red print, cut 2 strips 6½″ wide and as long as the long sides of quilt top. Sew to sides of quilt, using a ¼″ seam. Cut 2 more 6½″-wide strips the length of the top (or bottom) of quilt, including the side borders. Stitch to top and bottom of quilt.

9. Press quilt top and complete, following the directions in Chapter 4, "Putting It All Together." Quilt by hand or machine. This quilt's borders are quilted as previously described and illustrated, with feathers and triangles. Each red rectangle and gold square and *each* tiny square of each nine-patch block is quilted with an X.

10. Bind quilt edges with gold fabric, using the method described in Chapter 4 for easing around corners.

More Ideas for Squares

Indian Designs

Donna Rabe, a quilter penpal, has created a series of beautiful quilts using as her starting point

Figure 9-5. Three rows of "Nine from Gwen."

Figure 9-6. This charted Indian design makes a perfect quilt.

☐ White ■ Black ▨ Red 🔲 Yellow ▨ Avocado

▨ Turquoise

the copyright-free designs in *Full-Color American Indian Designs for Needlepoint Rugs,* a Dover Publications book written by Dorothy P. Story. Donna used black, white, red, yellow, turquoise, and avocado to make the quilt she calls "Apache II," following a chart like the one illustrated in Figure 9-6.

Cross-Stitch Clues

You don't have to limit yourself to Indian designs. Many simple charts for cross-stitch, plastic canvas, and needlepoint can be adapted to square-based quilt designs. Use some ideas from Chapter 7, "Triangle Tricks" to help you create the half-squares needed for some cross-stitch designs.

Charm Quilts:

A charm quilt is made with one template only, using each fabric only once. Traditionally, a charm quilt had 999 different pieces. That meant 999 different fabrics. Also known as beggar's quilts and odd fellers, these quilts are great fun for the viewer. You'll swear you can spot two fabrics

Figure 9-7. Many cross-stitch charts can be modified for use as quilt patterns.

alike, but on closer examination, they're different. A story is told in *Quilter's Newsletter Magazine* (No. 198, January 1988) of two little girls who, in 1893, invited neighborhood children in to try to find duplicate patches in a charm quilt. These enterprising young ladies charged the kids a nickel for this entertainment, until one girl's mother, the owner of this quilt, put the quietus on their moneymaking scheme. Needless to say, babies and young children are fascinated with charm quilts. (So am I, and if you'd like to send me a 4″ square of any red or red print fabric, I'll stitch it into my own ongoing creation. Sign or decorate it if you like, and send it to me. My address is listed in Sources of Supply at the end of the book.)

Most charm quilts are not made with squares, it's true, but the square is as valid a template as any to use in making these wonderful quilts.

Irish Chain

These quilts are made with several sizes of squares. They look best with an uneven number of Irish Chain blocks (for example, five); in that way, all four corners of the quilt are identical. A single Irish Chain begins as a basic nine-patch. alternated with plain blocks (see Figure 9-8).

Double Irish Chain starts out as a five-patch. The five-patch block alternates with an almost-plain block that has a square patch appliquéd or inserted into the corners (or it could be assembled with strips and squares). This easy pattern is pictured in Figure 9-9.

If you like this traditional pattern, look for triple Irish Chain and even more intricate versions.

Biscuits, or Puffs

This is a two-square technique. The base square, invisible in the finished quilt, is cut

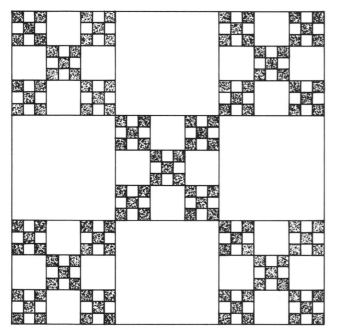

Figure 9-8. Single Irish Chain.

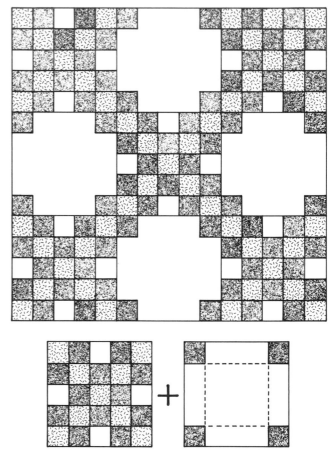

Figure 9-9. Combine two blocks for a double Irish Chain.

Figure 9-10. *The quilted cover gives* Easy Biscuit Quilting *that down-comforter look. (Photograph courtesy of Doris Carmack.)*

smaller than the top square. For instance, cut a 4″ square from some trash fabric for your base. Cut a 5″ square of patchwork fabric for the top. Stitch the 5″ square to the smaller square, wrong sides together, matching edges and pleating once on each side to make the squares fit. When you're stitching the fourth side, tuck in a bit of stuffing and finish sewing the side together. The squares are not turned. When you've made a lot of these units, stitch them together just as you would regular squares. You'll want to line a biscuit quilt, but no further quilting or batting is needed. These have a very luxurious, down-comforter feel and look to them. I learned everything I know about biscuit quilts from Doris Carmack's *Easy Biscuit Quilting* (see Sources of Supply).

CHAPTER TEN

LOG CABIN

The Log Cabin quilt design is traditional and versatile, and it is one of my two all-time favorites. When I interview myself, I ask, "If you could make quilts of only one design for the rest of your life, which design would you choose?" Sometimes I answer, "Trip Around the World"; sometimes I reply, "Log Cabin." I never choose Mariner's Compass or New York Beauty or complicated patterns. I'm more excited about combining colors and fabrics than I am about perfecting the pieced point or the masterpiece curved seam.

Making Log Cabin blocks is simple and foolproof. After you've made a number of blocks, you can begin the arrangement process, and believe me, this is fun. Unlike arranging cut squares, you're playing with modules that are visually complex to begin with.

First let's talk about how to make a log cabin block; then we'll discuss some of the possible arrangements. We'll talk about Star Trick, in particular, and then go on to some Log Cabin variations.

For beginners, I think Ma's method is best. Ma pieced almost everything on a base of trash fabric. This has three distinct advantages: It guarantees that all your blocks will turn out the same size; you can vary your seam widths to suit the idiosyncrasies of your fabrics; and it uses up trash fabric at a satisfying rate. Piecing to a base square is less intimidating, as well, because it's easier to cover a square than to construct one. Then, too, you may find that with the base layer and all the seams involved in Log Cabin piecing you can omit the layer of batting and still produce a comfy, warm quilt.

Figure 10-1. Fred and I made this Log Cabin quilt as a wedding present for our friends Charlie Davis and Randel Young. Fred quickly mastered cutting and breezed right into sewing blocks.

What do you use for your base fabric? Old sheets are fine if you don't plan to hand quilt—and Log Cabin is not the best design for an inexperienced hand quilter. Muslin is OK, too. Any light- to medium-weight cotton fabric is fine. You can even use printed fabric if the design doesn't show through your lightest color of Log Cabin fabric. Cotton flannel is excellent because the nap holds the fabrics in place and the weight is perfect for a warm quilt with no batting.

Let's start with a generous-sized square, say 12″. If you make 16 of these blocks, you'll have enough to play with. The more blocks, of course, the more fun. If you have sewing experience, you

can use 8″ blocks, make lots more of them, and produce more exciting designs. But for now let's assume a 12″ block.

Lay a ruler across your base block, corner to corner, and mark the center with an X. If you're planning on making your blocks right away, use a fade-away marker. You *can* use a pencil, but I will offer a warning that the pencil may show through. "Star Trick" (see color section, Figure 7) has some squares with red centers and some with yellow. A clever design addition, sure to appeal to babies, is the fringed center square, straight-stitched over the regular center square. These cute little squares transform a fairly common quilt into an artistic expression. Why did I add them? It wasn't planned originally. They were added to

Figure 10-2. "Sparkling Diamonds."

Figure 10-3. "Birds in Flight."

Figure 10-5. "Barn Raising."

cover up the X marks, made in good, soft pencil lead, that showed through the yellow cotton squares. The red was dark and dense enough not to allow show-through. We'll encounter many more design "opportunities," both in this book and in our quilting lives. Appreciate them when they enter your work.

The basic Log Cabin block results in a square made up of two triangles—usually one side lighter and one side darker. You can vary the width of

Figure 10-4. "Streak of Lightning."

Figure 10-6. "Star Trick." (Photo by author.)

your strips—in one block, I mean. It's OK. If you get out to the edge and the base square isn't quite covered by the strips, just trim the base square to fit. If the strips go over, that's all right, too. Just keep all your blocks the same size. There's almost no way to mess up a log cabin block or quilt. If you're the first to mess one up, I want to hear all the details. Your center squares can be almost any size as well. The more fabrics you incorporate into this, the better it looks. Figures 10-1 through 10-5 show some arrangements you can play around with in addition to our so-easy "Star Trick" design, explained in detail below (see Figure 10-6).

Quilt 4:
Star Trick

Materials

About 2 yards of trash fabric (can be muslin, flannel, or whatever); about 2 yards of backing fabric of your choice; scraps or ¼-yard cuts of the following fabrics: solid bright yellow, solid red, several yellow prints, several light-blue prints, several dark- to medium-blue prints; sewing thread to match fabrics; ¼ yard of binding fabric of your choice (Star Trick uses yellow satin); low-loft polyester batting

Tools

Rotary cutter and mat; scissors; straightedge; pencil, fade-away marker, or wash-out marker; hand-sewing needle (optional)

Finished Size

40″ square

Directions

1. Wash and dry fabrics; press if needed. If you're using scraps for your Log-Cabin piecing, you don't have to wash small pieces.

2. Using scissors or rotary cutter, cut your trash fabric into sixteen 12″ squares; set aside. Cut sixteen 3″ squares, 8 in solid red and 8 in solid bright yellow. Cut your blue and yellow prints into 1½″-wide strips of any length (this step is best done with the rotary cutter and mat).

3. Mark centers of base squares.

4. Lay a yellow center square onto the center of the base square, right side up. You know it's centered if each corner lies on a line of the X. Lay one of your shorter light-yellow print strips on top of it, right side down. Stitch and trim as shown in Figure 10-7. Open strip out to right side and press it flat with your fingers.

5. Lay another light-yellow print strip right side down on top of the square-strip combination as shown. Stitch, trim, and finger-press. (The X mark doesn't show in Figure 10-7 because it has already been covered.)

6. Now sew on a light-blue strip, followed by another. This establishes the colors for the entire block. Keep sewing yellow strips to the yellow sides and light blue to the blue sides until the base square is covered. Set square aside and make three more.

7. Following these same steps, make 8 squares with red centers, using your dark-blue prints and more yellow print strips. Finally, make 4 squares with yellow centers, using all yellow strips. You can vary the all-yellow look by dividing the strips into dark and light and using dark for one side, light for the other.

8. Press all your squares from the back. If your X marks show through, just cut smaller yellow squares, straight-stitch them over the center squares, and fringe the edges. If your X marks

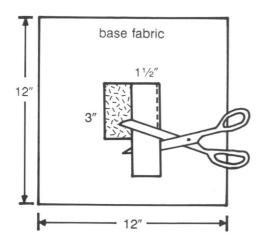

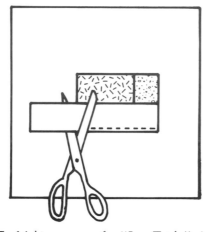

Figure 10-7. Making squares for "Star Trick." A. Cut after stitching. B. Continue adding strips: 2 light, 2 dark, and so on.

Figure 10-8. Adjacent strips of the same fabric don't look good (top). More life and interest is created when two light or two dark strips that meet are cut from different fabrics (bottom).

don't show, you might want to add the extra centers anyway, just for general interest and because babies like threads.

9. Arrange your big squares to form a blue star, referring to the color section for placement. Sew 4 squares together in a row, and press seams open; repeat for other 4 rows. Sew rows together; press entire quilt.

10. Complete quilt, following the directions in Chapter 4, "Putting It All Together."

Notes: Later, when you're making lots of blocks for a Log Cabin quilt, take this little tip. After you've made a few blocks, lay them together in a tentative arrangement. You'll find that if your blocks are identical, you'll wind up with two strips of the same fabric touching. This isn't usually good because the two strips look like one strip cut too wide. All you have to do is remember to use different fabrics for those last long strips, and you'll be in fine shape.

Log Cabin Variations:

Here are some just-as-easy variations on the basic Log Cabin block:

■ You can start with your square in the corner, then add 2 darks, 2 lights, 2 darks, and so on to the other corner. This kind of block, shown at the left in Figure 10-9, is generally known as a Chevron. Ma's quilt shown in Figure 10-10 is made from Chevron blocks.

■ You can start with your square in the center, as usual. Then add 2 logs to either side of it, 2 logs above and below those, 2 more logs on the

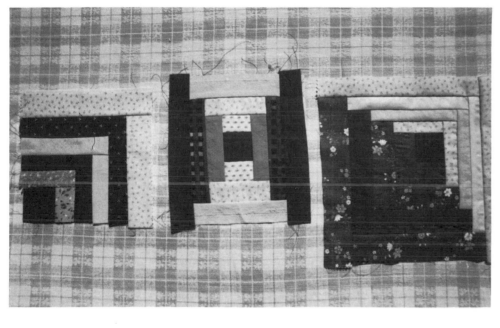

Figure 10-9. (left to right) Chevron Courthouse Steps, Off-center.

Figure 10-10. Ma's Chevron-style flannel baby quilt kept Evan warm.

sides, and so on until the base square is covered. This arrangement is called Courthouse Steps and is pictured in the center of Figure 10-9.

- Using off-center Log Cabin blocks produces the effect of curved lines rather than a simple diagonal. For example, you could cut all your dark strips 1″ wide and all your light strips 2″ wide, and you would wind up with a block that looks something like that pictured on the right in Figure 10-9. Placing 4 such blocks with the wide strips together makes a circle (well, sort of), and arranging them with the narrow logs adjacent looks something like a four-pointed star. The strip widths I suggest are quite arbitrary, and you'll have fun seeing just how this variation works.

- Instead of beginning with a plain square, make the center of each Log Cabin block a pieced nine-patch or four-patch block. Or begin with a printed or embroidered square and build up around it.

Figure 10-11. Golda Cooper's Log Cabin baby quilt. (Photograph by author.)

CHAPTER ELEVEN

STRIPS, STRINGS, AND STRIPES

Strip quilting ranges from the ultra-simple to the fantastically sophisticated. We'll take a look at some of the possibilities and explore several of the levels of the craft.

The two basic methods for strip piecing, just as for constructing a Log Cabin block, involve stitching one strip to another or covering a base block with stitched-on strips.

Figure 11-1. This easy strip quilt is from Kaye Wood's book, Quilt Like a Pro. *(Photograph courtesy of Kaye Wood.)*

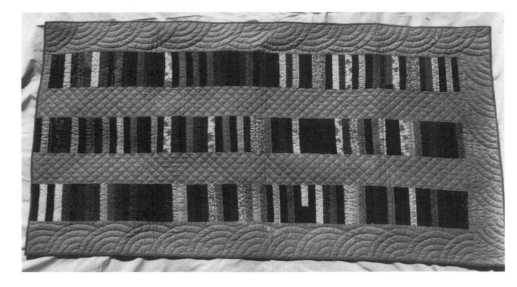

Figure 11-2. "Chinese Coins."

Quilt 5:
Chinese Coins

Gwen Marston and Joe Cunningham's Chinese Coins quilt (see color section, Figure 9), is a beautiful example of simple strip piecing using the first method mentioned above. Gwen and Joe travel and present workshops, lectures, and seminars. They also hold annual quilting retreats on Beaver Island in Lake Michigan. I was fortunate to attend one of these. Upon every bed in the dormitory is a quilt Joe and Gwen have made. That's how we picked our bunks—by choosing our favorite quilts. After a class at one of these retreats, Gwen (obviously a fabric lover) picked up the scraps the class members had allowed to fall to the floor. She cut the fabrics into strips, stitched them together, and created three strip-pieced panels. Gwen then added the bubble-gum pink solid panels, and she and Joe worked their magical hand quilting across the pink areas.

I first met these folks through their video series. They've produced five videotapes about quiltmaking, and I was not only educated but entertained by them. When I went to Beaver Island in September of 1988, I found Joe and Gwen to be as warm, funny, and wise in real life

as they were on videotape. In addition to their quiltmaking, writing, designing, and historical documentation, Gwen and Joe also make music. In fact, they first met through musical endeavors. When Joe expressed a desire to see more of Gwen after their project was completed, she told him that he would be more than welcome to visit—if he'd learn to quilt. He did, and a precious partnership was born. Every year, for Joe's birthday, Gwen pieces him a quilt top, and, she says, "Joe can quilt it any way he wants to." Having seen the fruits of their work, I can promise you that Joe quilts it absolutely beautifully. (There's more about Gwen and Joe in Chapter 9, along with their nine-patch quilt.) Chinese Coins is a traditional name for this pattern, and it's also known as a railroad quilt. I can see the railroad reference. Why the other name? I don't know.

Here's how you can make your own Chinese Coins quilt:

Materials
45"-wide cotton or cotton-blend fabrics as follows: 2 yards of solid-color or little pink print, 2

yards of backing fabric of your choice (Gwen and Joe's quilt is backed with a subtle beige print), $\frac{1}{2}$ yard of binding fabric of your choice (more if you cut on bias), lots of scraps; a 36″ × 67″ piece of low-loft batting; sewing thread; quilting thread (optional)

Tools

Sewing machine, scissors or rotary cutter, and mat

Finished size

36″ × 67″

Directions

1. Wash and dry fabrics; press if needed.

2. Cut scraps into strips about $1\frac{1}{2}$″ wide. Slight variation is OK. Strips can be any length over 6″, or you can piece strips together to achieve that length.

3. Seam strips together along the long edges; cut into 6″ segments. Make three strip-pieced panels 6″ wide and 68″ long. Press.

4. Cut pink fabric into four strips $5\frac{1}{2}$″ wide and 68″ long. If you have to piece it, that's OK.

5. Sew pink strips to strip-pieced panels. Press.

6. Assemble quilt as explained in Chapter 4, "Putting It All Together."

7. Quilt by hand or by machine. The quilt pictured is hand quilted as follows: Across each strip about $\frac{1}{4}$″ inch from seam, the inner pink strips are

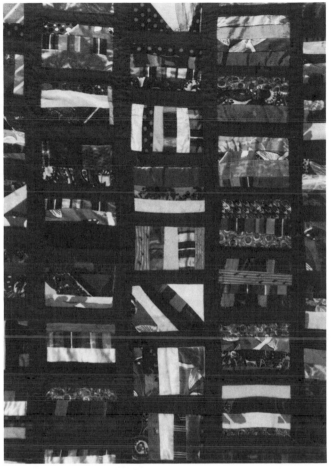

Figure 11-3. "Too Much Fun." (Photograph by author.)

quilted in 1″ diamonds, the outer pink strips in a clamshell design.

8. Cut binding about $1\frac{1}{4}$″ wide. Bind quilt following the directions in Chapter 4, using the method for easing around corners.

Quilt 6:
Too Much Fun

Some quilts just make you want to smile. This is one of those quilts. It is string-quilted and is pieced recklessly to squares or near-squares of trash fabric. Its riotous colors, bits of shimmer and shine, and absolute freedom are uplifting. You look at it and know that the woman who made it had herself some fun. The woman was my grandmother, Annie Taylor, and she lived in Wewoka, Oklahoma.

I lived with Ma and Pa until I was old enough

to go to school, then returned every June to spend the summer in their little house on the edge of town. Wild dewberries grew in profusion in the surrounding countryside, guarded by an occasional attack bull. Pa's garden produced an abundance of fresh food, and my life there was full of such luxury. When the summer sun shone too warmly on my treehouse in the big elm tree, I packed up my dolls and books and moved to the treehouse in the box elder tree. By the time the sun had found me there, the elm tree would be cool and shady again. The joy the viewer suspects in this quiltmaker is a verified fact.

I inherited several of Ma's quilts, although she gave most of them to the poor and to the Indians. Ma died without having quilted this top, and Golda gave it to me. For several years I just "collected" this quilt, but finally I undertook to quilt it. I took awhile to find the perfect fabric for the back, but I believe I found it. (See color section, Figure 10.) I had never hand quilted before, and I had no clues whatsoever. I basted those layers together as if I suspected an Oklahoma tornado were about to tear it away from me. That was one well-basted quilt! The first winter I tried quilting in a hoop. My stitches were wild and erratic, and I quilted maybe one quarter of the surface before summer's heat diminished my interest. It lay in the chest a few more seasons.

One winter I just quilted on it with no frame or hoop at all, and that really was not such a bad method. I had made friends with a famous and successful quilter, Sonya Lee Barrington of San Francisco, and Sonya told me that she just quilts in her lap without a hoop. That was a radical concept for me. I wasn't intimidated by this quilt, because Ma herself wasn't the world's best hand quilter, and she had pieced the top in her later years. Some of the seams didn't quite meet, and I had to reinforce the fabric here and there. So I felt as if I were being true to the medium, as it were. I don't know why it took so long to finish.

Finally, in the autumn of 1988, I bought a Quick-Snap frame, and I was hooked. Hand quilting became desirable fun. I turned on the television and made friends with David Letterman, the English comics, and other denizens of the dark hours. That quilt was finished in no time at all. Bound in red satin, there it is—a multigeneration endeavor. Ma, like the Afro-American quiltmakers, could and did work with odd and irregular shapes. Let us gloss over that, however, and pretend that these blocks and sashing strips are sensible in their measurements and angles; that way, I'll be able to tell you how to make such a quilt yourself. We'll also pretend that this is a baby-sized, rather than full-sized, quilt.

Caryl Bryer Fallert (about whom I'll tell more later) clarified for me the distinction between strip and string piecing. I'd always thought of the two as being similar in technique, with strips being wider and strings being narrower. Caryl says, though, "In strip piecing, all the strips are sewn together to make a new fabric. A template is then used to cut shapes from the strip-pieced fabric. In string piecing, the template is cut from paper, and the strips are sewn directly to the template, allowing for unlimited changes in angle, color and width of strips." If we extrapolate from that, what I call "Ma's Method" is string

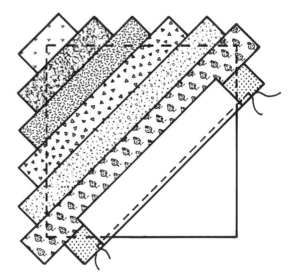

Figure 11-4. String piecing.

piecing rather than strip piecing, although she (and we, by extension, if we're following many of my directions) used fabric as a template rather than paper.

String piecing to a base fabric is a perfect baby quilt technique. It makes a good, strong quilt, and the multitude of fabrics is sure to entrance Baby. Strips can be of any width whatsoever, and you can use bigger pieces in the corners without cutting them into narrow strips.

Materials

About 2 yards of trash fabric for base squares, about 1 yard of teal blue for sashing, about 2 yards of backing fabric of your choice, about 1 yard of binding fabric of your choice (I used red satin), lots of scraps, low-loft batting the size you want the finished quilt to be, sewing thread, quilting thread (optional)

Tools

Sewing machine, scissors or rotary cutter and mat, quilting needle and frame (optional)

Finished Size

This is a full-sized quilt; 60″ square is recommended, give or take a little either way.

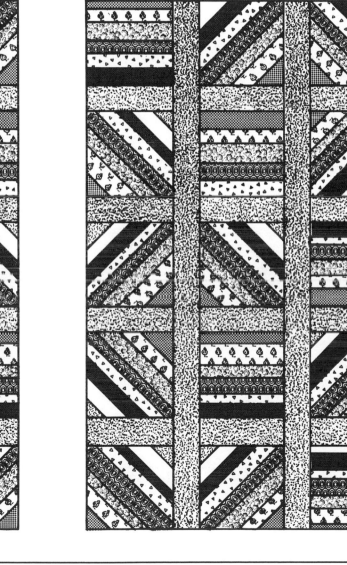

Figure 11-5. Sashing.

Directions

1. Wash and dry sashing and backing fabric. Wash and dry scraps that are large enough. Cut base fabric into 5″ × 7″ rectangles.

2. Cover base fabric with string piecing. Lay one strip down along an edge, right side up. Cover with second strip, right side down, and stitch through all three layers. Flip second strip to right

Figure 11-6. "Passion IV," by Nancy Crow, is composed largely of strip-pieced elements. (Photograph by J. Kevin Fitzsimons, Columbus, Ohio.)

side; press with your fingers to flatten out seam and lay next strip along edge of second strip. Stitch again. Continue until all rectangles are covered. Strips need not be straight, and they can be stitched down vertically, horizontally, diagonally, or just plain askew. Use the standard $\frac{1}{4}''$ seam on closely woven cottons; feel free to use a wider seam on satins, silkies, rayons, or mystery fabrics.

3. Cut sashing fabric into strips about 2″ wide.

Sew the shorter strips to the string-pieced blocks as shown in Figure 11-5. After you've joined enough blocks to make the quilt as wide or long as you want it to be, join another strip of blocks and sashing. Join these rows with long sashing strips in between. Press thoroughly.

4. Assemble quilt as explained in Chapter Four, "Putting It All Together." Quilt by hand or machine. I hand quilted with navy blue thread about $\frac{1}{4}''$ from the edges of the sashing. Bind quilt edges.

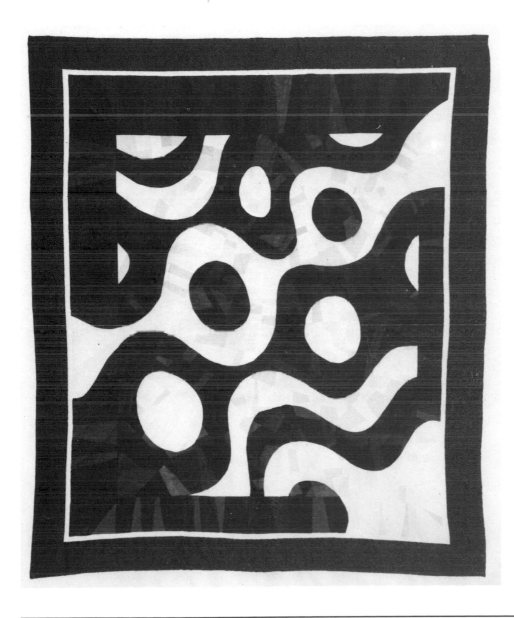

Figure 11-7. Strip quilts can be as complex as Caryl Bryer Fallert's "Rio Sidewalks." For this piece, black and white fabrics were crazy-pieced by machine to paper patterns; the paper was later removed. Quilting was done by machine. (Photograph courtesy of Caryl Bryer Fallert.)

Sophisticated Strips and Strings

I read in a newspaper article that one famous and successful quilter, Michael James, has an assistant named Florence Dionne. Her job is to assemble strip-quilted panels for Mr. James to use as a starting point for his art quilts.

Nancy Crow, whose striking quilts tour the nation's museums and shows, works largely with strip-quilted elements.

Caryl Bryer Fallert uses strip and string-piecing techniques in her work, which is characterized by swirling shapes and hand-dyed cottons. She works almost exclusively on the sewing machine for both the piecing and the quilting steps.

So we learn: A strip-quilted block is fine in and of itself; the block can be cut apart and reassembled; or the "block" doesn't even have to be a block—it can be an amorphous shape.

CHAPTER TWELVE
MORE IDEAS FOR STRIPS

This chapter could easily get out of hand; there's an entire book's worth of material floating on just the top layer of the possibilities here. We'll take a quick, cautious look at some of the myriad of designs that can come out of the simplest strip-piecing techniques, both "in the air" and pieced to a base fabric.

Herringbone

Cut base strips as long or as wide as you want the finished quilt to be. Cut or tear patchwork strips into different widths—or into all the same width. Stitch strips to the base fabric on the diagonal, then sew covered strips together in alternating directions. You'll wind up with a herringbone pattern without having to worry about those stretchy bias edges. The straight grain of the base strips stabilizes it all well enough to keep it on track. You can draw some guidelines on the base fabric if you want all your angles to coincide for a neat look. Stitch devil-may-care for a free-form folk-art effect.

Pinwheels

Cut your basic square pattern in half, then cut each half from a different fabric. Stitch 4 reassembled squares together as shown in Figure 12-2 to form a pinwheel pattern. It doesn't take very many of these blocks to produce an exciting quilt, especially if you choose striking, contrasting colors or mix two prints. Or, use one fabric throughout the quilt for one color and vary the other colors so that the pinwheel predominates

Figure 12-1. Herringbone pattern.

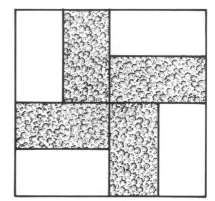

Figure 12-2. Pinwheel.

and the background recedes. Speedy method: Stitch long strips of the two fabrics first, then cut into segments.

Bargello Ribbons

Strip-piece several fabrics together. Stitch top and bottom to form a circle. Flatten circle and cut into segments. Cut one circular segment (a loop, we'll call it) apart at random, or else pick out a seam to form a flat strip. Lay strip out for a "starting place." Arrange the second strip so that the pattern is staggered up or down from the first strip; cut the loop at the appropriate place; and sew resulting strip to first strip. Continue holding circular segments to sewn-together piece, staggering seam lines up or down, and cutting the loop apart and sewing it in place. You can achieve breathtaking effects with this method. It isn't

fast, but it's quite easy, and you can use up *all* your thread making one of these.

Hitting the Bricks

Amazingly enough, you can make a fine-looking quilt with just rectangles offset like a brick wall. These quilts are commonly known as brick quilts, and they're so easy. Brick quilts are excellent for using up your scraps—or just showcasing them. Cut lots of different fabrics into rectangles, and cut a few of them in half for the end bricks on alternate rows. Then start stitching.

Tunnel of Love

Louise Townsend's beautiful "Tunnel of Love" quilt (see color section, Figure 11) is done in a way that is similar to the Bargello Ribbons technique, although Louise didn't use the circular loop-cutting method. I saw this quilt pictured in *Quilter's Newsletter Magazine* (No. 209, February 1989; see the Publications List at the end of this book) and thought it was outstanding. Now, it's true that Louise used hand-dyed fabrics and hand quilted a delicate heart-and-ribbons motif in each of the shorter segments. But even if you choose to use regular commercial fabrics and omit the quilting, you'll still come up with a striking and very easy quilt.

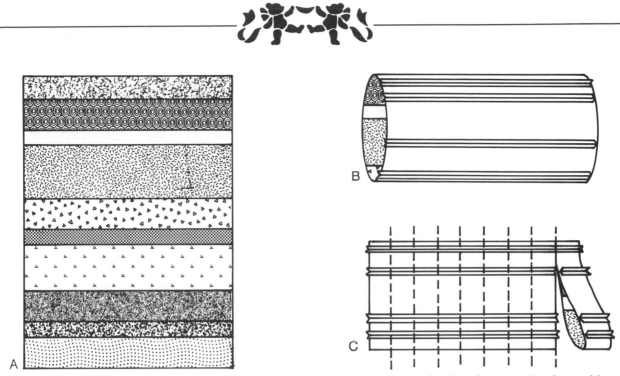

Figure 12-3. Bargello Ribbons. A. Strip-piece a panel of fabric. B. Sew panel end-to-end to form loop. C. Cut flattened loop into segments.

Louise planned and cut her strips, then assembled each vertical segment. Next she laid out her backing fabric, covered it with batting, and placed the first and second strips on as shown in Figure 12-6. After pinning, she stitched through all layers, then flipped the second strip to the right side. Each succeeding strip was added in this way, so that the quilt was already quilted when it was assembled. After stitching down all the strips, Louise added top and bottom borders in the same

Figure 12-4. Brick quilt.

Figure 12-5. Brick quilts can be very beautiful. Carolyn Martin designed this quilt. (Photograph courtesy PSC Publications.)

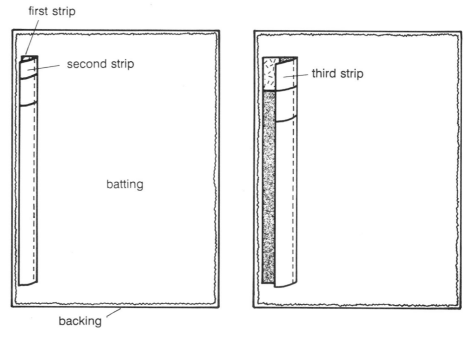

Figure 12-6. How Louise Townsend's "Tunnel of Love" quilt was constructed.

manner. Then she added the binding before hand quilting the hearts.

Louise says,

I came up with the idea on Thursday night, cut out the strips on Friday night, sewed the quilt together (including the binding) over the weekend, and then had one work week of evenings plus a weekend to do the quilting. It was definitely a "quickie" project! The name of the quilt turned out to be a slight misnomer. I used the word "tunnel" because I was under the impression that I was doing tunnel (or channel) quilting. However, I later realized that tunnel quilting uses strips of fabric both front and back, along with strips of batting; my quilt has strips on the front, but the batting and lining are both single large pieces. So mine is really a "flip and sew" method of quilting.

Louise goes on to say that *Quilter's Newsletter* has published articles of hers on no-mark quilting, using masking tape and Con-Tac paper (No. 189), and no-mark signatures, using basted tissue paper (No. 214).

Ladder of Success

Here's another ultra-easy quilt pattern using just strips. Although Ladder of Success is a traditional pattern, it's seldom seen. To make this pattern, begin by sewing shorter strips together to form

rows the length (or width) of the quilt. Join these with longer strips at right angles. Although if you make this quilt from multicolor strips you wind up with a Chinese Coins or railroad quilt, if you use just two colors this quilt design takes on its own identity and looks as if half of the shorter strips are appliquéd.

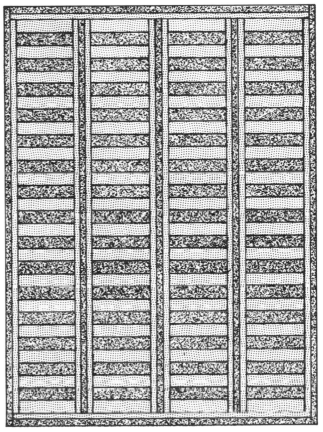

Figure 12-7. Ladder of success quilt.

Quilt 7:
Start with Stripes

Here's a tricky design developed by my friend Jahala in Sarasota, Florida. It does involve some bias seams, so take care in sewing those. Otherwise, it's a very easy technique that produces an impressive quilt. Similar to strip piecing, this method leaves most of the work to the fabric manufacturer.

Materials

One fabric with stripes of even width, sewing thread, batting, backing fabric

Tools

Scissors or rotary cutter and mat, sewing machine

Directions

1. Wash and dry your striped fabric and the fabric you've chosen for backing. Press if necessary.

2. Lay out your striped fabric and study it. Cut a strip with stripes running lengthwise. Make sure the end is square, then fold the bottom corner up to the top edge. Press and cut along both the diagonal and the vertical.

3. Now fold the resulting triangles in half and cut again. Stitch triangles together.

4. After you have cut and reassembled 16 such triangles to form 4 blocks, you'll find that each set of 4 blocks will produce 2 identical blocks and 2 contrasting blocks. They'll look something like the blocks shown in Figure 12-9.

5. Now you're pretty much on your own. If you're not entirely happy with your 4 blocks, cut stripes with different sequences and repeat Steps 2 and 3 to get a different set of 4 blocks. Repeat these steps when you've found the perfect arrangement. Make as many blocks as you like.

6. Stitch blocks together in rows, then sew the rows together. Complete quilt assembly following the directions in Chapter 4, "Putting It All Together."

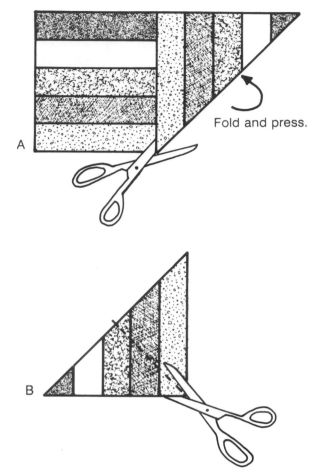

Figure 12-8. Cutting striped strips into triangles. A. Cut along fold. B. Cut resulting triangle in half.

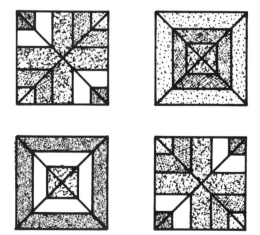

Figure 12-9. Four variations from triangles.

Figure 12-10. One possible outcome of Jahala's "Start with Stripes."

CHAPTER THIRTEEN
APPLIQUÉ TODAY

Appliqué today paints a whole different picture from yesterday's time-consuming, hand-stitched methods. Like hand quilting, hand appliqué is absolutely beautiful. Even people who do it well, though, would probably agree that it's not the best baby-quilt technique. Save hand appliqué for home-decorating items and adult clothing, and instead explore some of the sturdier, quicker, bolder ways to embellish your baby quilt with appliqué.

Quilts in this chapter utilize machine-appliquéd crocheted doilies and other motifs ("Victorian Fantasy") and basic satin-stitch machine appliqué ("Baby's Big Brother" and "Dinosaur Parade."). There's also faced appliqué (my big-time favorite), faced and padded appliqué, dimensional appliqué in regular woven fabric as well as Ultrasuede, and a neat new technique invented by Jeannie Spears that she calls "Appli-fray." All these techniques are worked into "Dinosaur Parade," an appliqué sampler that almost ran away with me.

The aforementioned Jeannie Spears is a multitalented Minnesotan. She is editor of *The Professional Quilter* magazine, author of *Mastering the Basics of Quiltmaking,* and publisher of Oliver Press. In her spare time, Jeannie travels and teaches and makes quilts, of course. She specializes in hand-dyed, hand-quilted pieces, and she markets patterns for fantasy creatures like dragons. Jeannie's address is listed in the Sources of Supply section at the end of this book.

There are uses of appliqué mentioned in other sections of this book. "Country Baby" in Chapter 14 exploits the frayable qualities of

Figure 13-1. Cute and easy—Jahala's appliquéd teddy. Purchased fabric machine appliquéd to front and back of quilt. Add simple borders.

denim to make quick-and-easy straight-stitch appliqués. Janet Sylvain's colorful "Pocket Pals" quilt in Chapter 16 has a bit of appliqué, as does Cory's "New Rosie," a quilt that features big flannel roses hand appliquéd after being faced and stuffed. All these are shown in the color section.

In addition to the specific techniques used for the quilts in this chapter, there are many more methods for appliqué that lend themselves to baby quilts. Here are some lifted straight from Robbie and Tony Fanning's *The Complete Book of Machine Quilting* (see the Book List at the end of this book). They're given here in an abbreviated, casual form. This is a tiny, tiny sample of just a few pages on one topic—I highly recommend the entire book.

Appliqué Methods

Straight Stitch

1. Turn under a ¼″ seam allowance and topstitch along the edge.

2. Face the appliqué shape (this process is described in the directions for "Dinosaur Parade") and appliqué with straight stitch.

3. Stitch ¼″ from edges and let them fray.

4. Straight stitch over and over again in close, semi-parallel rows.

Open Zigzag Stitch

1. Zigzag fabrics that don't fray. Never mind about turning under edges.

2. Turn under seam allowance and zigzag along the edge.

3. Stitch once around the edge, then zigzag cording, pearl cotton, or other trim around the edge.

4. Set machine for blind hemstitch so that the stitch just catches the appliqué motif.

Satin Stitch

1. Use fabric glue or glue stick around edges; back with typing paper to stabilize before stitching.

2. Trace design on appliqué fabric; cut out a large shape around the design. Pin loose shape to background fabric and straight stitch in place first. Trim fabric close to stitching, then satin stitch.

3. Stabilize back of appliqué fabric with iron-on interfacing. Draw design on appliqué fabric; then cut out design and pin to background fabric. Pin interfacing behind background, then satin stitch.

4. Fuse paper-backed webbing like Wonder-Under to appliqué fabric. Pull off paper and fuse appliqué to foundation. Satin stitch or zigzag edges.

5. Mark design on wrong side of background fabric. Pin piece of appliqué fabric bigger than design to front of background. Stitch around marks on background with narrow zigzag. Turn over, trim appliqué fabric away outside zigzag stitching line. Satin stitch from top side.

Now—on to specific quilts on which you can practice some of these techniques.

Quilt 8:
Victorian Fantasy

Years ago I machine appliquéd an old crocheted doily to the front of a sweatshirt. The shirt never received any special consideration; in fact, it was one of those things you wear at least once a week and wind up wearing to bathe the dog. Much to my surprise, the crochet appliqué never showed signs of fraying, fading (it was a two-color piece), or coming unstitched. I made another for myself and several for gifts. This was no fluke; machine appliquéing crocheted doilies is a safe and sturdy technique.

The narrow zigzag stitch recommended for the appliqué blends in perfectly with the crochet, and the stitches become almost invisible. Best of all, if your doily (or other motif) is used and has come unstitched in places, the narrow zigzag stitch that bonds it to the flat base serves as a stabilizer, filling in any blank places and strengthening the crochet against any further deterioration.

Although I found these crocheted pieces in Ma's collection, there's no way of knowing whether she was the crocheter or not. She'd take anything anybody wanted to give her and would give you anything she had. I can recognize her quilts in a crowd, of course, but who can say about a piece of crochet? If you don't have access to a mixed bag of crochet motifs, not to worry. Garage sales, thrift stores, and quilt shows generally have them for sale quite reasonably. Chances are that some of your friends or relatives have old bits of crochet tucked away that they'd be glad to share if you just spread the word. And, if all else fails, you can buy new crocheted motifs at craft stores. Best of all, of course, would be pieces crocheted by one of the new baby's ancestors. Interview the baby's mother, grandmother, or aunts if you want to make this type of quilt.

Using big squares and this easy zigzag method, you'll be able to assemble this quilt in a very short time. I used high-loft batting and yarn ties to hold it together (see color section, Figure 12).

Figure 12. "Victorian Fantasy" features crocheted doilies machine appliquéd to big squares.

Figure 13. Karen Montgomery and her designer-colleague Brandon Montgomery created "Baby's Big Brother." Such a quilt provides a way for bigger kids to welcome a new arrival.

Figure 14. "Dinosaur Parade" is a sampler of many appliqué styles.

Figure 17. "Country Baby," or "Matthew's Quilt" (opposite page). Rough-and-tumble fun in an easy appliquéd quilt.

Figure 18. ''Butterfly Squiggles'' is an example of free-motion quilting.

Figure 19. Janet Sylvain's ''Pocket Pals'' is colorful and fun. (Photograph courtesy of PSC Publications.)

Figure 20. Meryl Ann Butler's "Guardian Angel" quilt will guarantee sweet dreams.

Figure 21. Here's a way to use lamé and other sparkly fabrics in a wall quilt.

Figure 23. Bonnie Benjamin of Needlearts International designed this beginner's sashiko project. (Photograph courtesy of the artist.)

Figure 22. Layers of hearts held with Flexi-Braid and a button are perfect for a wall quilt.

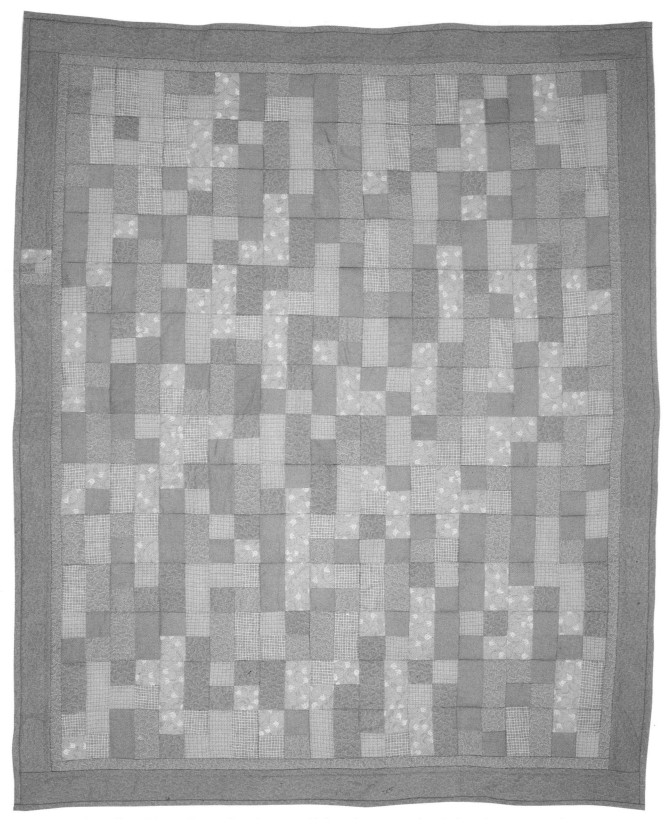

Figure 24. Alice Allen's "Sweet Dreams" quilt is assembled on the serger and quilted on the sewing machine.

Materials

25 rectangles of assorted pink fabrics measuring 11″ × 12″, 1½ yards of pink fabric for ruffle, one 52″ × 56″ piece of high-loft batting, 2 yards of backing fabric (this quilt is backed in solid rose pink), sewing thread, pink yarn for tying, 5 crochet motifs, pearl cotton or household string (optional)

Tools

Sewing machine with zigzag capability, large-eyed needle, scissors or rotary cutter and mat

Directions

1. Wash and dry your fabrics; press if necessary.

2. Cut an assortment of pink fabrics into 25 rectangles 11″ × 12″; arrange to suit your fancy.

3. Determine which squares will have appliquéd crocheted motifs and decide how to place motifs to the best design advantage. (Although the lacy effect of the crochet shows up best on solid-color fabrics, I was tempted by the textural interplay of crochet on a print fabric, too.)

4. Thread your sewing machine with top thread to match the crocheted piece. Bobbin thread color is not important. Set stitch width for a narrow zigzag with stitch length set at 12 stitches per inch or so. You don't want a dense, piled-up satin stitch here, just a spacy little zigzag.

5. Pin the doily to the fabric in several places and begin stitching. If the motif is large, you might want to begin near the center so that you can work out any fullness or ripples as you reach the outer edges. I just stitched these motifs around the edges, and they seem to be securely attached.

6. Sew quilt top together in rows; then sew the rows together. Press quilt top well and then cut backing to the same size as finished quilt top, adding an inch or two all around for insurance.

7. Cut ruffle fabric into strips 10″ wide, and seam together to make a loop. Fold the ruffle strip in half lengthwise with wrong sides facing.

8. Set your machine for a long, wide zigzag stitch. Thread color is unimportant. Lay the length of pearl cotton or household string along the raw edges of ruffle strip about ¼″ to ½″ from the edges. Zigzag over the string as shown in Figure 13-2a.

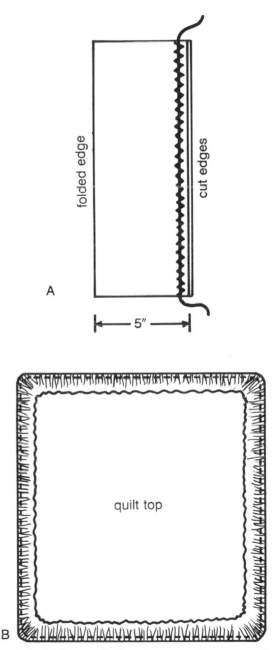

Figure 13-2. Making ruffle for "Victorian Fantasy" quilt.

Be careful not to catch the string in the stitching, which is quite easy to do if you're not paying close attention.

9. Pull up the string to form gathers. Gather ruffle evenly into a loop to measure around the quilt-top edges. Trim corners of quilt to round slightly. Pin ruffle to quilt top as shown in Figure 13-2b, allowing a little more fullness of ruffle at rounded corners. Machine baste ruffle to quilt top.

10. Lay quilt backing wrong side up on quilt top, with ruffle sandwiched in between. Shorten stitch length to a normal stitch to sew layers together. Even though the ruffle is hidden under the backing fabric as you sew, you'll be able to sew neatly over it because it's basted in place, and you can feel it easily through the backing fabric. Start sewing along one short edge just before a corner. Sew around that corner, around all three sides, and around the fourth corner. Stop stitching, leaving most of one short edge open. Turn quilt to right side.

11. Lay batting out on quilt and trim to match. (Be careful not to snip your quilt!) Fold batting a couple of times and insert it into the open side of quilt. Reach in and flatten it out neatly. Sew open side of quilt closed, stitching by hand or by machine.

12. Tie quilt with pink yarn at intersections of squares or rectangles, tying knots on front or back of quilt, depending on your preference (see Chapter 4). I decided these knots should be on the back.

> *Notes:* Cutting your fabric in squares rather than rectangles would produce an equally attractive quilt. My first square turned out to be a rectangle instead, and of course I took that as a sign from the cosmos and cut all rectangles. This quilt would also look good machine quilted in the ditch.

Quilt 9:
Baby's Big Brother

Or big sister. This is a quilt to be designed by the older sibling to welcome and, in a sense, to educate the new baby. The older child is going to be jealous from time to time, but investing his or her artistic effort in a gift for this helpless little creature can only produce more tolerance for the inconveniences the new baby brings. And when you show respect for the older child's contributions and artistic creations, that child's self-esteem takes a healthy giant step forward. If the new baby is yours, the time you spend working with your older child on this type of quilt strengthens your relationship and may provide the first experience in a new relationship—that of collaborators, colleagues.

Karen Montgomery made this quilt after we'd talked about the concept of the older child showing the new baby things he'd need to know (this is our house, our car, our cat). Karen has created lots of other things with her children and with their art, such as free-hand stitchery, crayon painting, and, mostly, her machine-appliquéd versions of her children, Brandon and Lauren's, artwork.

For this quilt, Brandon first drew the center panel, based on the family's home in Davie, Florida. Then he drew the items in the surrounding panels, things that would be important to the baby. These are all sashed together with a blue glazed cotton print and then machine quilted (see

Figure 13-3. "Baby's Big Brother," made for the newest family member.

Figure 13-4. Detail.

color section, Figure 13). Here's how to make your own version of Karen Montgomery's quilt, "Baby's Big Brother."

Materials

A child who'll draw and design for you; fabric as follows: about 2 yards of blue cotton print, 1 yard of white cotton or muslin, 2 yards of backing fabric (this quilt is backed with white cotton); a 42″ × 50″ piece of low-loft quilt batting; lots of scraps; sewing thread in assorted colors including blue to match fabric; freezer paper; fusible appliqué webbing

Tools

Sewing machine with zigzag-stitch capability, scissors, rotary cutter and mat (optional), iron, basic art supplies

Directions

1. Decide on size you want your appliqué blocks to be. Cut pieces of freezer paper to that size. (If your child tends to draw small figures with lots of space around them, trim paper larger than you want block to be; if she draws right up to the edge, trim paper a little smaller.) Karen Montgomery's quilt has 6″ (finished) blocks and a center block that measures 18″ × 24″.

2. Find a comfortable spot where you and your child can draw, color, and paint. Do your pictures of things you think the baby would be interested in. You can draw right on the matte side of the freezer paper if you like. If you don't want to cut up the child's original drawing, you can trace over the lines to make a pattern you can cut out.

3. Read the beginning of this chapter for a short course in basic machine appliqué. That's all the instruction you'll need for this quilt. Karen uses the freezer paper as an embroidery and machine-appliqué stabilizer as well as for drawing the pattern. Iron the shiny side of the paper to the wrong side of appliqué background.

4. Wash and dry fabrics; press if needed.

5. Cut a 19″ × 17″ piece of solid-blue or blue-and-white print and a 9″ × 19″ piece of green fabric. Seam together along the 19″ sides with a ½″ seam. Press seam toward the green side. This forms the base for your center panel.

6. From white or muslin, cut twelve 7″ squares (or whatever size you've decided on).

7. Trace drawings or cut up the originals for patterns. Cut out major shapes. For instance, for a cat cut the shape of the face from the fabric chosen for the cat. Then cut out eyes and nose from appropriate fabric, then pupils of eyes. Work from large to small pieces so you won't have to keep tracing your patterns.

8. Follow the manufacturer's directions to fuse webbing to wrong side of appliqué fabrics. Some of these products come with a paper backing, while others use a combination of webbing and a Teflon sheet. There are many choices available, and you won't have any trouble finding a good product at your local store or through the mail-order sources listed at the end of this book.

9. Appliqué smaller shapes to larger ones; then appliqué larger shapes to blocks. Where two shapes come together (like the tree leaves and the tree trunk), you may want to cut a little extra and lap one shape over the other as you fuse.

10. Print words with wash-out or fade-away marker or with pencil. Machine embroider over letters with the same width of zigzag satin stitch you used for machine appliqué.

11. Check size and shape of appliquéd blocks; they can become a little distorted with all the stitching. Trim evenly if needed and press.

12. Cut blue print fabric into several 3½″-wide strips and 8 squares the same size as your smaller appliquéd blocks.

13. Arrange blocks as you like. Sew a blue square between 2 of the smaller blocks to go at bottom of quilt. Repeat for the 2 blocks for top of quilt.

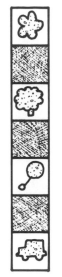

Figure 13-5. Assembling strips from plain blocks and appliquéd blocks for "Baby's Big Brother" quilt.

Press. Now sew 4 appliquéd blocks to 3 plain blocks for side of quilt and repeat for other side. See Figure 13-5.

14. Sew 3½″ strips to assembled-square strips as shown in Figure 13-6.

15. Sew strip/square combinations to center medallion. Sew 3½″ strips to all four sides of quilt for borders. Press quilt top thoroughly.

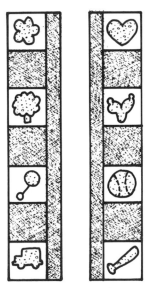
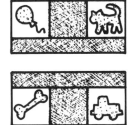

Figure 13-6. Sewing plain strips to block strips.

16. Assemble quilt as explained in Chapter 4, "Putting It All Together." Quilt by hand or machine, or tie at corners of blocks. Karen's quilt is machine quilted ¼″ from each block, and as follows: around the outline of the house, along the green-blue horizon line in the center block, and along the curved line of the sun. Borders are also quilted ¼″ from inner seams.

17. Round corners of quilt and bind with bias strips of the blue print fabric.

> *Note:* When I told my good friend Barbara Hayes about this quilt, she reacted strongly. "I'm doing one!" she said. "I'm collecting drawings from the kids in the family and doing a quilt for Kirk's sister." I went over to Barb's to see the work in progress, and little Beth met me at the door to show off her new red coat (that Barbara, of course, had made for her). Beth also wanted to show me her doll quilt. She had drawn the pictures, and Barbara had machine appliquéd them for her (see page 114).

Quilt 10:
Dinosaur Parade

Beginning as a simple sampler of appliqué techniques, this piece quickly escalated. Without all the restraint I could muster, it could have become a sampler of everything I know how to do in fabric. Fortunately, I subdued it just in time. It's still ridiculous and extravagant, but you can eliminate lots of the details and still come up with a neat little quilt (see color section, Figure 14).

Use all four of the dinosaur patterns, as I did, or discard one and make a three-panel quilt. These creatures, incidentally, are ideal for your first appliqué project because no one can tell you that it doesn't look right. A dinosaur can be any color you want, have any proportions, any kind of feet or scales, and can bulge or sag anywhere. Except for the dinosaurs themselves, almost everything in this quilt is optional, but here's how this one was made. The colorful fake ikat strip near the horizon line was one of the ugliest fabrics I ever bought on impulse. I bought way too much, but it was cheap—and doesn't it make good water

reflections? I'd hate to see a dress made out of it, though.

Materials

Patterns for dinosaurs, lots of scrap fabrics or ¼-yard cuts in different greens and blues for background, scraps or 15″ squares of solid-color fabrics for dinosaurs, 12″ square of solid-color yellow fabric for sun, several floral prints with big isolated flowers, scraps of leaf prints with big isolated leaves or scraps of green or blue-green Ultrasuede, 2½ yards of trash fabric for base, 2 yards of 45″-wide backing fabric of your choice (this quilt is backed with some of the same solid purple fabric the first dinosaur is cut from, plus a muted plaid with flowers on it), sewing thread including some to match dinosaurs, one 45″ × 65″ piece of quilt batting, additional pieces of batting if you want to pad some of your appliqué pieces, tiny scraps of white felt or Ultrasuede for eyes, scraps of Ultrasuede for spikes (add to as many of the dino-

Figure 13-7. "Dinosaur Parade" (detail).

saurs as you like), tracing paper to make dinosaur patterns (can be regular-size typing paper, but you'll have to use a bit of tape), fusible appliqué aid (this can be a paper like Aleene's or Wonder-Under, or fusible webbing and a Teflon sheet; in either case, follow the package directions for use)

Tools

Sewing machine with zigzag stitch, scissors, rotary cutter and mat (optional), 10″ to 12″ plate or something similar to cut circle for sun, iron

Directions

1. Wash, dry, and press larger pieces of fabric. Don't bother going through all this for the tiny bits.

2. Trace dinosaur patterns from book. Just trace the big shape, then lay that over the head or feet or tail and complete the shape. Draw casually. Dinosaurs are not like horses; that is, they don't have to look a certain way.

3. Cut base fabric into strips 45″ long and wide enough to hold dinosaurs comfortably—the length of the dinosaur plus 5″ is fine. Strips for this quilt before sewing measured from $16\frac{1}{2}$″ to $17\frac{1}{2}$″ wide. Strips can vary in width or be all the same; it doesn't matter. Cut blues and greens for background in strips of varying widths and at least as long as the base strip is wide (or 18″ long, to be on the safe side). I planned a wide solid-color strip as background on which to place each dinosaur, but that's not mandatory. Using the big strip makes the dinosaur show up better and prevents seam ridges from showing through the appliqué.

4. Decide where you want the dinosaurs to go. In my quilt the dinosaurs are spaced at different levels. Their feet are from 7″ to 12″ from the cut bottom edge of each strip. Mark foot placement on base fabric with light pencil or fade-away marker. Mark horizon line as well. On my quilt foot placement is 25″ from the cut bottom edge. Strip-piece green fabric up to foot placement. Add wide strip for dinosaur background, then continue strip piecing greens up to horizon. To simulate distance, use darker shades of green cut in narrower strips as you approach the horizon.

5. Optional mountains: Cut two 4″ × 18″ rectangles from dark purple, gray, or navy blue fabric. Lay rectangles right sides together and stitch an arbitrary wavy or jagged line as shown in Figure 13-12, beginning and ending near the corners. Cut $\frac{1}{4}$″ from stitching along one side. Sew $\frac{1}{4}$″ from wavy cut edge of the leftover two pieces. Clip curves. Turn both mountain pieces to the right

Figure 13-8. Dinosaur 1: Match A to A, B to B, C to C, D to D, and E to E to complete pattern. Dotted lines indicate satin-stitch detail.

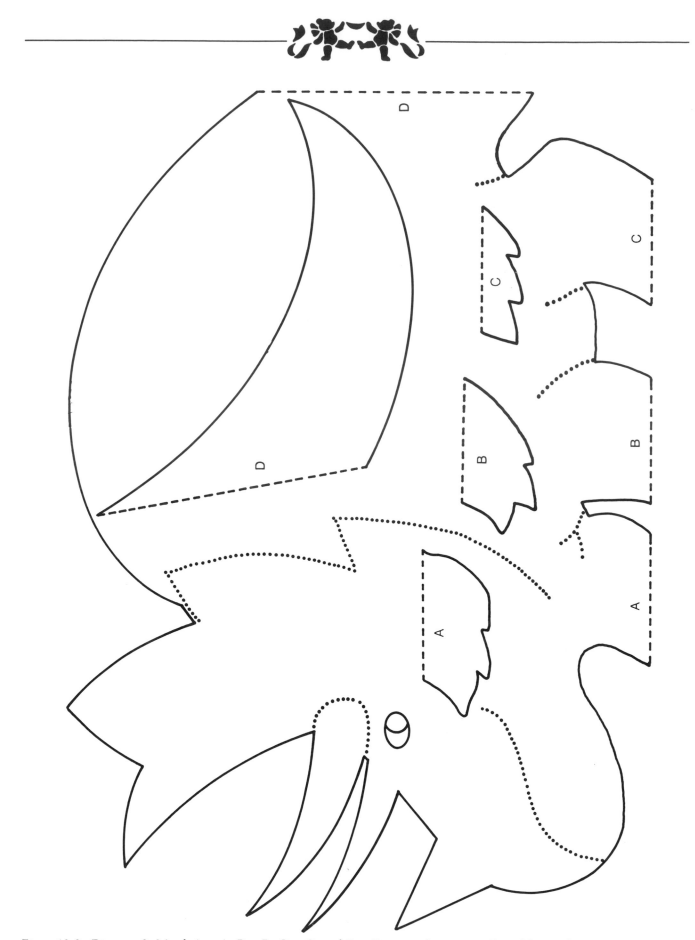

Figure 13-9. Dinosaur 2: Match A to A, B to B, C to C, and D to D to complete pattern. Dotted lines indicate satin-stitch detail.

Figure 13-10. Dinosaur 3: Match A to A and B to B to complete pattern. Dotted lines indicate satin-stitch detail.

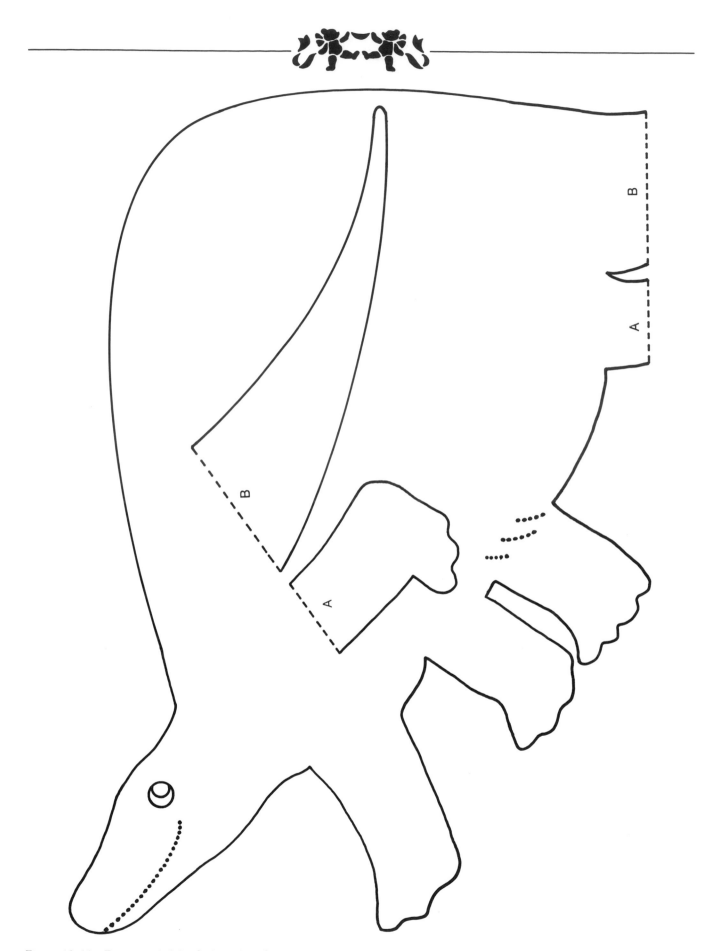

Figure 13-11. Dinosaur 4: Match A to A and B to B to complete pattern. Dotted lines indicate satin-stitch detail.

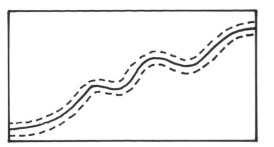

Figure 13-12. Making mountains for "Dinosaur Parade." Stitch, cut, and then stitch again.

side and press. If you want only one mountain range, discard leftover pieces. When sewing first sky strip to last ground strip, tuck in the raw cut edges of the mountain piece and sew through all layers. Mountain will just hang there; so, after you're finished with the background strips, you'll have to take a couple of stitches by hand or machine to sew it to the sky and make it look right (see Figure 13-13).

6. Continue strip piecing until remainder of strip is covered with blue. Press all strips thoroughly from the wrong side. Set strips aside.

7. Lay a piece of muslin or other white or yellow fabric on the right side of yellow fabric for sun. Trace around a plate or other 10″ to 12″ circle onto the backing fabric. Stitch right over that traced line all the way around the circle. Cut $\frac{1}{4}″$ outside stitching, then clip little triangles out of the seam allowance so curve will lie flat. Pinch up a bit of the backing fabric and cut a slit 4″ (or so)

long in it. *Cut the slit through backing fabric only; don't cut yellow sun fabric.* Through this slit, turn the circle right side out. Press from the wrong side. Lay on batting and cut out a circle of the batting. Trim $\frac{1}{4}″$ or so from circumference. Roll up batting, slip inside slit, and flatten out to pad circle. Set sun aside.

8. Cut a loosely shaped piece of appliqué fabric for each dinosaur. See Figure 13-14. Follow package directions to apply fusible webbing to wrong side of appliqué fabric. Pin paper pattern to fabric. Trace around outline first, if you like, or just cut shape out with scissors. One of these dinosaurs has Ultrasuede feet; two have Ultrasuede spike-things down their backs. If you want these things, cut them out, free-form. Tentatively lay dinosaur on panel; position feet or spikes or other additions underneath. Carefully lay dinosaur back in place Again following package directions, fuse appliqués to strip-pieced panels.

9. Thread machine with thread color that more or less matches the dinosaur. Set machine for medium-to-wide satin stitch. If your machine has a satin stitch or open-toe foot, put it on. Make a practice line of stitching. If any of your bobbin

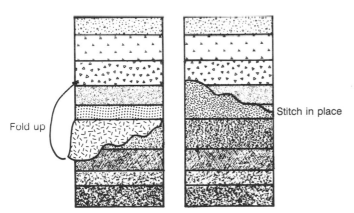

Figure 13-13. Attaching mountains for "Dinosaur Parade."

Fold up

Stitch in place

Figure 13-14. Cut appliqué fabric just big enough to contain dinosaur.

thread shows on the top, loosen top tension just a little and make another practice line. It's OK if top thread shows underneath. Stitch all around dinosaur, then stitch little design lines. If you feel really good about this, try tapering your satin stitch, widening and narrowing it here and there to sculpt the body more.

10. Cut tiny circles of white felt or Ultrasuede for eyes. Sew them on in the center of the eye with black thread and a wide satin stitch. This theoretically looks like dinosaur eyes with *black* pupils.

11. Pin two panels together, matching the horizon line. Nothing else needs to match, and you can always trim top and bottom edges, so don't worry about them. Sew remaining two panels together in the same way, then sew middle seam, always pinning and matching at horizon. Press seams open.

12. Sew sun in place by hand or machine. I set the machine for free-motion quilting and then drew around a glass for a smaller center circle. I quilted around that circle, then made free-motion petal-like shapes with the smaller circle as a center.

13. Make faced appliqué flowers and leaves as follows: Cut out flowers, cutting an inch or so outside the motif. Lay right side of flower down on backing fabric. (Backing fabric should enjoy a pleasant visual relationship with flower fabric if appliqué will not be stitched down around the edges; otherwise it doesn't matter.) Sew right along edge of flower motif or a scant $\frac{1}{8}''$ outside it. Clip curves and corners. Pinch up backing fabric and cut a slit in backing fabric only. This is the same procedure used to stitch, trim, and slit the sun circle. Turn flower to right side through slit and press. Make as many flowers like this as you want.

14. Make faced and padded appliqué flowers and leaves. Add a layer of batting just as you did to make the sun; and, of course, you can add more in places to sculpt some flowers.

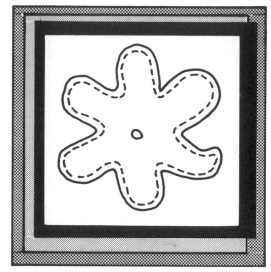

Figure 13-15. *Stitch through all layers.*

15. Make Appli-fray flowers (if desired) as follows: Place a flower motif right side up on 3 layers of loosely cut fabric. Stitch through all layers, then trim fabric just outside flower motif (see Figures 13-15 and 13-16). Trim second layer $\frac{1}{4}''$ larger, third layer $\frac{1}{4}''$ larger than that, and so on. Jeannie Spears invented this method, and she just stitched her layers together in a very casual spiral line of stitches. I stitched mine more cautiously, and Charlie has drawn it even more carefully. But this careful stitching is not at all necessary—just ask Jeannie. Fray edges by pulling out threads, or

Figure 13-16. *Trim layers.*

toss completed flower assembly into washer and dryer with some corresponding color laundry to fray automatically. Make as many flowers like this as you want.

16. Make Ultrasuede leaves as follows: Cut as many leaves as you like from as many colors as you want. Cut shapes as complex as you like, because you will sew them to the quilt with one line of stitching (you don't have to appliqué around the edges).

17. Place leaves and flowers anywhere you like on quilt. Flowers can just float in the air, for instance. That's OK; we don't know whether flowers drifted in the air at the time of the dinosaurs or not. Maybe they did. If there are any little discrepancies in your quilt top, cover them with a flower or leaf. There's no need to plan the placement; if you do, it will be a nuisance to pin all the leaves and flowers in place. Just start sewing. Some different ways to appliqué these motifs are given in Step 18.

18. Sew faced appliqués (as well as faced and padded appliqués) either around the edges or just in the middle, leaving petals free. See Figure 13-18, which, again, is drawn more carefully than you will need to stitch. Sew Appli-Fray appliqués in place over first stitching lines, or almost any way you fancy. Sew Ultrasuede leaves to quilt top in single lines, as if the sewing lines were veins in the leaf. Add more tributary vein lines if you like, or if the leaf is very large.

19. Complete quilt assembly as explained in Chapter 4, "Putting It All Together." Since we're having true confessions here, I'll admit that I had trouble letting this quilt go. I hand quilted some rays from the sun, quilted around the leaves in the upper left-hand portion, and quilted a few horizontal lines along the strip-pieced areas. Then I got really silly and pieced the binding to correspond with the strip piecing of the quilt. (Could this be a cosmological clue to the disappearance of the dinosaurs? Did they just ornament and overwork themselves into extinction?) I had fused my webbing to the wrong side of one of my little creatures, and he didn't look right in the parade, so I just appliquéd him to the quilt backing rather than toss him out.

Figure 13-17. Appli-fray flower before raveling. (Photograph by author).

Figure 13-18. Sewing appliqués. Stitch in the center, or near the edges (dotted lines).

CHAPTER FOURTEEN
SPECIAL FABRICS

We develop preferences and feelings about weaves and weights of fabrics that can be as strong as our feelings about color. Explore different fabrics in your work, and you'll learn a lot about what they will and won't do. A baby quilt, or any smallish piece, is a good project on which to learn the qualities of fabric. You can find out whether you're happy sewing velveteen or satin, or if the lines on gingham help you get your strips pieced straighter. "Opti-Dots" (Chapter 8) contains silk, but it's a sturdy quilt. "Star Trick" (Chapter 10) has little fringed squares sewn to it. That ravelly linen was perfect for those little squares. You can use almost anything if it is good-quality fabric and you know what to do with it.

In addition to gingham and denim, which we'll get into more deeply in a few minutes, you may be lured by lamé, curious about corduroy, swayed by Ultrasuede. Let's talk about the qualities of some of these. Obviously, quilters most often choose to work with 100% cotton broadcloth for good reason; they're not just being narrow-minded. When you forsake this practical fabric for the shine, the nap, the gleam, and the glitter of other fabrics, you pay a price. Some of these enticing fabrics are discussed below.

Corduroy

It's soft and pretty. It washes and dries like a dream. So what's the problem here? It creeps all over the place. It's hard to piece accurately, and even harder to machine quilt. I wouldn't even consider hand quilting the stuff. I've made two all-corduroy quilts, choosing to surmount these difficulties, and I love them both. If you choose to work with corduroy, make simple designs like "New Bluebird," for which matching isn't a problem. Machine quilt with a walking foot or else just tie the quilt. Once you've made the corduroy quilt, it's perfect for babies. It's just the doing that's difficult.

Lace

I've used sturdy cotton lace (both as lace-edging embellishment and as cut squares in a pieced design) in baby quilts with good results. Although lace doesn't invite the touch, it can be used to produce an intriguing look.

Lamé

There are two kinds of lamé on the market: woven and tricot-backed. Both shimmer and shine and look fabulous. Neither is very cuddly; lamé has a cold feel to it. The tricot-backed kind won't ravel, but you stand a great risk of melting it if you even wave an iron near it. Put plainly: *Do not press tricot-backed lamé.* The woven kind ravels wildly, but I just learned a trick. Iron fusible interfacing to the back of it, and it works just fine. Use either type in small amounts, as accents, for wall hangings. Neither will withstand frequent washing and drying.

Polyester

I quote a T-shirt Charlie gave me for my birthday one year: *Polyester nec nominetur in nobis.* The rough translation from the Latin: "Let polyester not be so much as spoken of among us." Oh, I know, Ultrasuede is some form of polyester. Like most prejudices, mine can be easily punched full of holes.

Rayon

Rayon can be tricky to sew with, does creep, feels good, is an almost-natural fiber, and comes in lovely colors and patterns. Major drawbacks: lacks strength and sometimes gets very wrinkly after a few launderings. Use only in small amounts, like in strip piecing.

Satin

Satin feels *so* good—but it's horribly grouchy to sew with because it has a mind of its own, and that mind is unbalanced. Also, satin doesn't stand up to much wear and tear or laundering. Why, then, do I use it for bindings so frequently? Because it's touchy-feely, and because bindings are simple enough to sew on the first time and easy enough to replace when worn.

Silk

I actually screeched when I saw my friend Judith Montaño toss her silk noil skirt into the washing machine. For all my fears and protests, she had shrugs. "I put it in the dryer, too," she deadpanned, enjoying it all. My basic belief system had just been challenged. But saying "silk" is like saying "cotton." Each basic fiber comes in

countless weaves, knits, textures, strengths, and so on.

In baby quilts, use only silk noil. It's a fairly rough-looking fabric, but it feels lush and soft to the touch. It takes dye beautifully, is easy to sew, withstands quite a bit of wear, and holds up in the laundry. Look for bargains, though. Prices range from $6 to $26 a yard. Of course, you can find 2 yards for a dollar if you're willing to scout the Goodwill store and cut a waistband off a skirt.

Ultrasuede

Ultrasuede feels good, looks good, and wears like some kind of synthetic iron. It's easy to sew, good for patches and embellishments, needs no hemming, and makes a grand binding. Price is the only major drawback, but if you use scraps, even that problem disappears. Sources for Ultrasuede scraps are listed at the back of this book (see Clotilde and Aardvark).

Velvet

Worse than velveteen for creeping, velvet doesn't hold up well. Velvet comes in rayon and silk. It is a beautiful fabric—but save it for something else.

Velveteen

Pretty much the same story here as with corduroy, although velveteen is even more luscious and touchable than corduroy. It's not quite as sturdy and long-lasting as corduroy, but it's tough enough. Velveteen comes in cotton and blends.

The baby who does have a velveteen quilt is very lucky. Use it, by all means, but don't try anything too tricky with it. How about using it for the back of a quilt? Or alternating big squares with plain cotton print? Or using it in strip piecing? All of these ideas would work fine.

Gingham

Gingham provides a woven-in gridwork that comes in handy when you're making quilts. In fact, for strip-piecing to a base fabric, you can't beat gingham for trash fabric. In addition to its use in Claire Field's beautiful tied star quilt, "Check It Out" (see color section, Figure 15), for which you'll find complete directions in the next section, gingham also lends itself well to pleating and tucking. By stitching either the dark or the light areas of the checkerboard, you can make one tone predominate.

Look for the February 1990 issue of *Crafts 'n Things*, which includes directions for LaRayne Meyer's gingham baby quilt. Meyer's quilt uses manipulated tucks in a clever way. Lines of machine stitching neatly divide the gingham into dark and light stripes; then the tucks are pressed in alternate directions for a shift in color. Nancy Tosh and Lois Dahl of *Crafts 'n Things* were nice enough to share a photograph of the quilt with us (see Figure 14-1), and you'll find subscription information in the Publications List at the end of this book.

Teneriffe embroidery—also known as snowflaking, chicken scratch, and mountain lace—is another good embellishment technique for gingham. It's often worked with white thread, with a double cross-stitch (a star) lightening the darkest squares and a wheel emphasizing the white ones. Figure 14-2 shows how simple the embroidery is. After filling in the dark checks with stars and the medium checks with spokes (just a single long straight stitch), you're ready to make the wheels around the white squares. To do that, bring your needle up near the end of the spoke and pass your thread under all 4 spokes twice; then return the thread to the wrong side of the fabric at the starting point.

If you like this idea but you're shy of hand

Figure 14-1. Tucked gingham quilt. (Photograph courtesy of Crafts 'n Things)

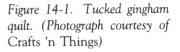

Figure 14-2. Teneriffe embroidery.

embroidery, see "More Ideas in Motion" in Chapter 15 for basic directions on how to do chicken scratch with your sewing machine.

You'll probably come up with some inventive gingham ideas of your own as you experiment with this classic fabric.

Quilt 11:
Check It Out

Some of us are in love with our sewing machines, and some of us are not. That's OK. For those of you who enjoy a quiet bit of handwork, here's a beautiful quilt technique that you can adapt in lots of ways. I found this quilt in the book *Tie It You'll Like It,* by Claire Field, and it is used here with her permission (see color section, Figure 15). This method transforms the tying step into

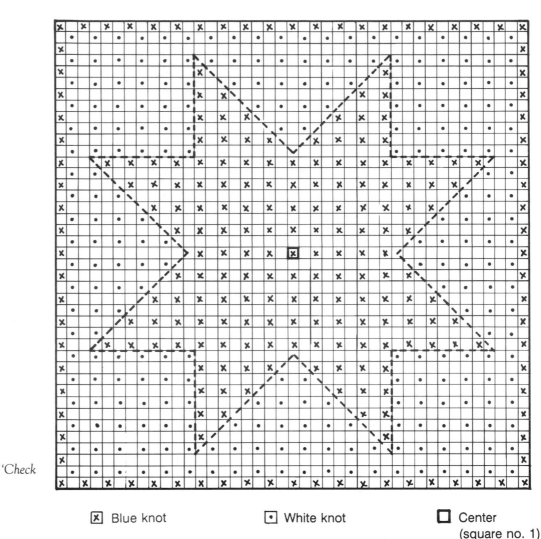

Figure 14-3. Chart for "Check It Out."

| ☒ Blue knot | ⊡ White knot | ☐ Center (square no. 1) |

the main visual message of the quilt. It's worked on gingham with 1″ squares.

You can order needles and the *Tie It* book, along with selected quilting supplies and patterns, from Claire. She also travels and gives lectures on quilting and sells custom-made quilts. Check the Sources of Supply list at the end of this book for more details.

Materials

Chart; 2 yards of 45″-wide blue-and-white gingham fabric with 1″ checks; 1¼ yards of backing fabric of your choice; a 45″ square piece of bonded quilt batting; 2 skeins of 4-ply acrylic yarn, 1 in white and 1 in royal blue; sewing thread to match fabric

Tools

No. 15 needle, sewing machine, scissors or rotary cutter and mat, wash-out or fade-away marker

Directions

1. Prewash fabrics and press them. Trim gingham to make a piece with 21 white squares horizontally and vertically and with a blue stripe around the edges. Cut the rest of the gingham into bias strips 2″ wide.

2. Fold gingham in half horizontally, then vertically, to find the center white square. Count that square as no. 1 and count 5 squares out from the center in all 4 directions; mark those squares with a wash-out or fade-away marker. At the end of each line, count 5 squares at angles as shown on the chart. Mark the complete star outline.

3. Lay your backing fabric out wrong side up on a flat surface, and then lay the batting over it. Over that, place the gingham top with the star outline facing up. You can either safety-pin the layers together, or you can baste the layers together with long hand stitches. In one of these ways, you need to hold the sandwich together temporarily while you tie the yarn.

4. *Inside* the star outline, tie square knots with blue yarn in the center of each white square. *Outside* the star outline, tie square knots with white yarn in the center of each dark blue square. Along the quilt edges, tie blue knots in the center of each white square.

Knot Notes: You can tie a plain square knot or any knot you like. Or, try this fast knot-tying method: Thread your no. 15 needle with enough doubled yarn to go across the quilt. Start at the right edge of the quilt (if you're left-handed, start at the left edge). Take a healthy stitch (between $\frac{1}{4}''$ and $\frac{1}{2}''$), with the mark on the square in the middle of the stitch. Tie the first knot by hand into a square knot: right over left, then left over right. Don't cut the yarn. Go to the next stitch placement and take another healthy stitch. Now "throw up" your yarn, cross over the strip of yarn, and go under into the loop. Pull very tight. (See Figure 14-4a.)

To complete knot, "throw down" yarn, cross over strip of yarn, and go under into loop. Pull very tight. (See Figure 14-4b.)

Continue stitching like this across the row of marks. Your tied knots will look like the knot shown in Figure 14-4c. Finally, cut the yarn between the knots. Once you're accustomed to tying this way, you'll be able to tie this square knot in a flash!

5. Sew the bias strips together into a continuous band and bind the quilt edges. If you like, you can also machine stitch around the outside of the star design.

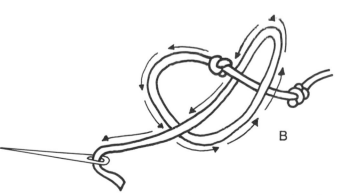

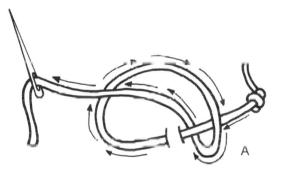

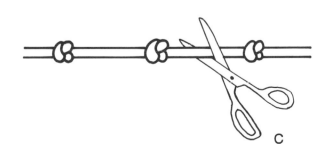

Figure 14-4. Tying knots the fast and easy way (arrows show direction of forming knot). A and B. Follow arrows to complete knot. C. Cut between knots.

Quilt 12:
Country Baby (Blue Denim)

My youngest, Evan, was born in a 100-year-old two-room adobe house high in the Sangre de Cristo mountains. There was no running water into the house (though it was piped up into a wellhouse in the backyard), and quite a few of our neighbors didn't even have the luxury of electricity (though we did).

Blue-jean quilts are perfect for babies like Evan. They're pure rough-and-tumble fun. Toss them onto the floor for Baby's crawling practice or onto the meadow grasses for his staring-at-clouds time. A blue-jean quilt is often the right choice for the first child of an extremely macho man, too. The quilt will stand up to years of car trips, tentmaking, and benign neglect. Also, if you've been putting off making a beloved child his or her own quilt for entirely too long, this quilt is equally appropriate for teenagers.

Blue-jean quilts aren't new in our family; Golda has made several. And I made denim curtains, filled with heavy batting, for Evan's room, to help his windows keep out winter chills. Evan now finds them quite suitable for maintaining the constant gloom favored by many of today's teens.

Recently I have been seeing denim-on-denim appliqué, raw edges fraying, held in place by only a single line of machine stitching. Most of this appliqué was on long prairie skirts or fringed vests, and the motifs selected were largely in the

Figure 14-5. "Country Baby" ("Matthew's Quilt"). (Photograph by author.)

current trendy Southwestern coyote-wearing-bandanna-baying-at-the-moon style.

But, I thought, why stop there? Why not make a real educational blue-jean quilt, incorporating tricky appliqué shapes that I'd never wrestle with if I had to turn under edges or even satin stitch? Thus I designed, for my brand-new-grandnephew, Matthew Alan Spakes, the quilt illustrated in Figure 14-6.

The theory behind the quilt is that each shape is found in the upper two rows of designs and repeated in the lower rows. It's a fine, workable idea—*if* one were using new denim yardage. That, however, is not my style, and I planned to use the old blue-jean collection, with its many faded hues of indigo. Thus, cutting squares of identical size and shape from my collection quickly proved to be too time-consuming and too wasteful of the resource. Instead, I cut the jeans into squares and rectangles of any size whatsoever, using as my criteria my knowledge of what a right angle looks like (no straight-edges or templates) and making the full use of the denim piece. This approach resulted in a wide array of

Figure 14-6. The original idea for "Matthew's Quilt."

pieces. I knew I couldn't piece these together in any traditional manner, so I opted for crazy-quilt methods, with no batting.

Materials

About 2 yards of backing fabric (Matthew's quilt is backed with red bandanna print), several pairs of old blue jeans in various stages of fading (for paler blues, soak denim in mixture of 1 part liquid chlorine bleach to 3 parts water; for darker blues you may have to buy new denim yardage), binding fabric ($\frac{1}{4}$ yard of regular woven fabric if cut on straight of grain, $\frac{1}{2}$ yard if cut on bias, about $\frac{1}{6}$ yard of Ultrasuede), 3 large spools of blue thread, 3 large spools of thread to match backing fabric, bandanna (optional)

Tools

Sewing machine, scissors

Directions

1. Wash and dry any new denim. Wash, dry, and press backing fabric.

2. Cut denim into largest possible squares, strips, and rectangles. Try to include at least one pocket. Save the smaller pieces for appliqué. Cut and piece backing fabric to the size you want the finished quilt to be. Matthew's quilt is 53″ by 51″.

3. Lay large pieces on backing just to get an idea of how many you need; don't pay attention to arrangement.

4. Cut out appliqué shapes, working freehand. As you cut each one, lay it on a larger piece of denim that contrasts and is right for size. Leave some pieces of denim blank.

5. Take your appliqué shapes and denim blocks to the sewing machine. Use blue for the top thread and a color to match your backing in the bobbin. Put a new denim (size 16) needle in your machine. Straight stitch around each motif about $\frac{1}{8}$″ from the cut edge, pivoting when necessary. Appliqué all your blocks.

6. Fold up what (arbitrarily) will be the right-hand portion of the quilt backing and safety-pin it together in 2 or 3 places (or use bicycle clips). Working from left to right will keep the biggest part of the quilt (most of the time, anyway) off to the left and out of your way.

7. Begin straight-stitching denim blocks to the backing fabric. If you're going to wrap your backing fabric around to the front for a binding, leave about 1″ of the backing unappliquéd all the way around. Otherwise, start right at the edge of the backing. Overlap the pieces ¼″ or so when you can. There will be pieces that won't quite meet. That's OK. You can go back later and fill these in much more easily than you can fiddle with them now. Cover the backing with denim blocks, working from left to right and safety-pinning the stitched left-hand portion of the quilt if and when it gets unwieldy. If you work on a big table, or set

a side table up to the left of your machine, you may not need to pin the quilt up. Take care in this step and the next that the weight of the quilt doesn't hang off the table and drag your stitching. Keep the fabric flowing freely under the needle.

8. Now satin stitch over all the straight stitches that join the blocks to make them prettier and stronger. Set your machine for the widest possible zigzag stitch and shorten the stitch length until it almost looks like satin stitch but not quite. A satin stitch is completely closed up, with no fabric showing between the stitches. This stitch is attractive, but it sometimes causes fabric to bunch up under the presser foot when you're working on bulky fabrics like denim. If your first line looks too open, you can stitch over it again and then shorten the stitch length a little. If your machine has a special satin-stitch foot, by all means use it here. If you feel the stitch beginning to pile up under the needle, you can nudge it along when the needle is in the "up" position. Don't try to push or pull the fabric while the stitch is being formed, though, or you could break the needle. Once all the stitching is done, tiny variances won't show up at all. This is a mindless step that takes a bit of time and yards of thread. Turn on the television or listen to books on tape (see Sources of Supply), and you won't even notice you're doing this step.

9. Fill in the inevitable little gaps with strips of denim or with bits of Ultrasuede. Satin stitch the denim; straight stitch the Ultrasuede.

10. Bind the quilt, following the directions in Chapter 4, "Putting It All Together." This quilt is bound with 1″ strips of Ultrasuede. I used scraps so my strips are of varied lengths. Because Ultrasuede doesn't ravel, you don't have to piece. Just overlap the strips slightly and add a new length. Also, you don't have to turn under any edges while stitching the binding to the quilt.

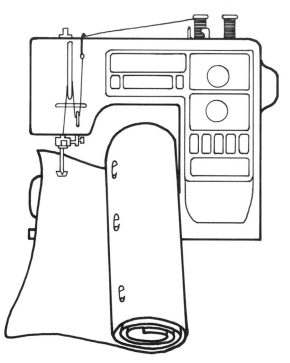

Figure 14-7. Keeping the quilt out of the way as you sew: roll up the right-hand part of quilt, then work left to right.

Note: To make the lacy doily effect, lay foil doilies on denim. Blot with sponge dipped in mixture of 1 part liquid chlorine bleach and 1 part water. This is not a scientific technique—sometimes you get almost-perfect lace doilies, and sometimes you get something like the earth floating through space.

You could also incorporate practice pieces of machine stitching (like your programmed stitches) or other embroidery on denim into your quilt. The white cat, worked in cross-stitch, is about the sum total of my cross-stitch experience.

Because everyone is comfortable with denim, you might encounter unexpected help on this quilt. I did. First Fred came through the room and, knowing the makings of a good time when he saw them, picked up some scraps and scissors.

Next Evan arrived and pitched in with the car, the peace sign, and the cross. It turned into a family evening, all right. I just had to remind them to keep the motifs simple, simpler, simplest. It's much easier to cut them than to sew them down.

I love the combination of blue denim and Ultrasuede and have used it in wearables. It's a perfect combo in this quilt because Ultrasuede matches denim for pure indestructability, and it's just as amenable to repeated laundering. Plus, it gives Baby a little touchy-feely in addition to the raised shapes of the denim appliqué.

If you look closely at the "Country Baby" quilt pictured in the color section (Figure 17), you'll notice that the binding is made up of many short pieces of Ultrasuede. There is absolutely no good reason for this. It is the sort of thing you do on a holiday weekend when you have scraps on hand and don't want to wait until you can drive into town and spend $10 for $\frac{1}{8}$ yard of Ultrasuede. Heck, I'd do it that way again.

CHAPTER FIFTEEN

OUR MARVELOUS MACHINES

Women have made baby quilts with the simplest needles and thimbles and threads. And a surprising number of today's exciting machine-embroidery techniques were developed on treadle sewing machines. Take a look at the 1911 *Singer Instructions for Art Embroidery and Lace Work.* You will be amazed. However, while we don't really *need* our machines, they can provide quite a bit of fun. In this chapter, we'll look at what you can do with a standard sewing machine, a quilting machine, and a serger.

Most of us who already own sewing machines have models that can produce a programmed stitch. Even a simple zigzag stitch can be manipulated—made wider, narrower, longer, or shorter; metallicized or rayonized.

You can combine making a baby quilt with familiarizing yourself with all these programmed possibilities. Cut a stack of 12″ squares, assemble your thread collection, and get out your sewing-machine manual. Spend an evening or an afternoon just playing. Don't like the look of one of those stitching lines? It doesn't matter. Nobody but the baby is going to focus on that one imperfect line, and she may find it her special favorite. It's the overall effect we're going for, and the overall effect is going to be fascinating.

When you've exhausted your stitches, threads, and ideas for that day (you'll think of more tomorrow), lay out your embellished squares. Stitch them together as is, or add sashing, or alternate the stitched squares with plain squares. You'll have a quilt top that will intrigue the curious eyes and fingers of any baby.

If you begin hanging out with quilters, you'll

cloth. There are times and places for such things. If you don't find it locally, check Sources of Supply at the end of this book (one source is listed, but I'm sure there are lots more out there). I had thought cheater cloth to be a fairly recent development until a few years ago when we cleaned out Golda's attic. There was an ancient, worn-to-shreds utility quilt made of cheater cloth in a red-and-white star pattern. The quilt had to be at least 40 years old.

Figure 15-2. Cheater cloth by Wamsutta Fabrics looks like pieced block.

Figure 15-1. Programmed stitches on stripes, sample by Vivian Luster.

soon hear the term "cheater cloth." Cheater cloth is fabric specially printed to look like an already-pieced quilt. You just do the quilting, by hand or machine, straight-line or free-motion. There is no disgrace involved in using cheater

Before we go on to talk about sergers and the special effects we can get with our home sewing machines, let's consider a machine with which you may not yet be familiar, the quilting machine. One of these babies would take up most of my living room. Charlie and I used to joke about buying one together ("You can keep it in your house." "Oh, no, I couldn't be so selfish—you keep it in *your* house."), but now it seems they're no joke. I've encountered several women recently who own their own quilting machines or are considering buying one. I'm certainly not suggesting that you purchase a quilting machine for your first baby quilt, but you might want to think about having that quilt machine-quilted on one in your area.

The woman I talked to the most extensively on the subject had bought such a machine, had almost mastered the operation of it, and was handing out business cards for her service. She showed me several quilts she'd done and told me that the machine had a capability of producing 10 or more quilting designs. None of these designs, frankly, was very exciting to me, and the quilting was obviously done by machine. Think of a mattress pad or a mass-produced quilted bedspread or comforter, and you get the picture of what the quilting machine does. But let's not turn up our collective noses.

My acquaintance said that she charged $1 per square foot of quilt and that she furnished the thread. Even my rudimentary math skills tell me that this is a very inexpensive way to complete a quilt. It seems ideal for baby quilts in particular, as it produces a sturdy and secure bonding of the layers. It is an option to keep in mind—and isn't that what we learned from the eighties?

Super Serging

If you already own a serger, you might as well use it for quiltmaking, too. Here's why: It stitches faster than your sewing machine, you never have to wind bobbins, it makes stronger seams (important in baby quilts), and it feeds the two layers of fabric through more evenly than your sewing machine does.

Wow! Then why would you *not* use such a terrific time-saving device? One good reason is that serged seams are bulkier than those made on a standard sewing machine.

Most people are terrified of sergers at first, so they waste a lot of time acting meek and mild. I was like that for awhile. I did the pull-thread-through method and serged all my picnic tablecloths. Then, figuring I was somehow ahead of the game, I put it up for a few weeks. One fine day I felt aggressive, so I took off the red-green-blue-yellow code threads and manually threaded that baby with serious gray thread all around the two needles and the two loopers. There have been several tense moments since then, but nothing terminal. Once you've made friends with your serger, you'll love it. Judge by your own tendencies. Are you computer-literate? Can you drive a standard-transmission automobile? No problem.

With a serged quilt, you can put the stitches to the inside or back of the quilt so that it looks like a normally sewn quilt, or you can flaunt them by turning them to the front. Here's a good place to use your shiny rayon embroidery threads in the loopers.

In addition to Alice Allen's "Sweet Dreams" quilt and my own "Pink Cloud," in the next section, you should take a look at the serged quilt in *Distinctive Serger Gifts & Crafts*, by Naomi Baker and Tammy Young (Chilton 1989). This quilt is made of satin, taffeta, and velveteen squares which are serge-tucked. The tucks are then stitched down in alternate directions, giving a glimpse of the contrasting color thread used on the reverse side—in the lower looper, that is. This is a beautiful piece of work, and the authors swear it's not that difficult.

Quilt 13:
Pink Cloud

My good friend and yoga teacher, Joanne Anderson, used to talk her classes through a marvelous relaxation sequence. We began with the tips of our toes and ended floating on a soft and welcoming pink cloud. I had that ultimate cloud in mind while designing, searching for fabric, and making this quilt. Although this one is pink (see color section, Figure 16), why not a blue cloud? Or any soft color, really, would produce that cloudlike look. You could even make it in reds and call it a rose or a poppy; the ruffles also look like petals. Or how about just white, with every conceivable color used on the serged edges?

Enough high-flown talk; this is an incredibly easy quilt. I made it before I took my serger class, and all settings remained the same throughout. You must have books on tape, old movies on the television, or some strong linear entertainment, or you will become bored. But in the process, you will become very comfortable with your serger. You will also use up lots of thread.

Materials

1½ yards of good-quality 45″-wide pink flannel, about 3½ yards of other varied 45″-wide pink fabrics, varied pink threads.

Note: This quilt is 45″ square, and has 30 pleated ruffles that are each 3″ wide. It required 6 small (225-yard) spools of rayon thread and 2 larger "mystery thread" spools of the same, along with 3 large spools of regular sewing thread. I used the rayon thread in the loopers and the sewing thread in the needles.

Tools

Rotary cutter and mat, sewing machine, serger, wash-out or fade-away marker, ruler

Directions

Note: Directions for many sewing projects call for cutting off the selvedges of fabric, and there's usually good reason for that. In this quilt, though, selvedges are our friends. There is no turned hem in the entire project. If an edge is not a selvedge, it's serged.

1. Wash and dry all fabrics.

2. The flannel will become the base of the quilt. Trim it evenly. Serge cut edges of flannel and set the flannel aside while you make the ruffles.

3. Cut your collection of pink fabrics into strips approximately 3″ wide across the width of the fabric so each strip end will be a selvedge edge. Cut 15 of these strips in half crossways so they are 3″ wide by about 22″ long.

4. Serge-seam the cut edge of your 30 half-strips to one end of each of 30 whole strips. This will give you 30 strips, each about 59″ or 60″ long and still having selvedges at both ends. (I say about, because your fabric may be 42″, 43″, 45″, or 48″ wide.)

5. Serge-overcast all the long cut sides of the ruffles. When you run out of one color of pink thread, just tie on another color and go right on. Variegated threads look good on this, too.

6. On the wrong (smooth) side of the flannel, mark off every 1½″. This will show you where the

center of each ruffle begins and ends. You can eyeball the rest of it, lining up each ruffle with the adjacent one.

7. That's all the serging; we'll finish on the sewing machine. Pin beginning and ending of first ruffle to the marks on what we'll arbitrarily call the far left of the quilt. Match center of ruffle strip to mark. You might want to look at the illustration for the "Country Baby" quilt in Chapter 14 and roll up the flannel base in this way. Pin this first ruffle to the quilt in several places. Set machine for a basting stitch. Sew the first ruffle in place, just folding a little of the fullness toward you as you sew. Go slowly with the folding and sewing on this first row; all the others will be fast and easy. If your pleats come out fairly evenly on this first row, change to a regular stitch length and re-sew. If you wound up with way too much at the end or no fullness at all, well, that's why we basted at first. Rip the basting out and try again. It doesn't have to be perfect at all; you'll get it right the second time.

8. Now you have an idea of how much to fold up per pleat. Pin the center of one end of the second ruffle to the second mark. Set machine for regular stitch length. On this ruffle, make the pleats in between the pleats on the first ruffle, and use about the same fullness. Magically, it will turn out right! Especially if, when you're about 15″ from the end of the seam line, you check the length remaining in the ruffle. You can cheat a little on the fullness from there to the edge, making the

pleats a little narrower, or skipping a pleat. You'll want to line up the center of the end of the ruffle strip with the second mark, anyway.

9. Continue sewing ruffles to the flannel backing. If you didn't start at the far left, and the ruffles get too bulky for ease, just turn the backing end for end and work out to the other side. The direction of the ruffles will change, but that's all right.

10. You'll probably have just enough ruffles to cover the flannel backing. If you have a few left over, you can save them for a future strip-quilting project or a binding. If you don't have quite enough, you can go back to the serger and either overcast a few more strips or run the too-long edge through again to trim and overcast. This shouldn't be too unwieldy a process.

11. You're done! No batting, no turning edges under, no quilting! Just a big fluffy, ruffly fantasy quilt and a big empty space on your thread rack.

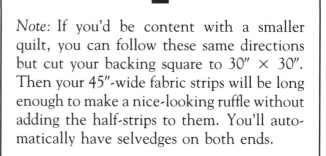

Note: If you'd be content with a smaller quilt, you can follow these same directions but cut your backing square to 30″ × 30″. Then your 45″-wide fabric strips will be long enough to make a nice-looking ruffle without adding the half-strips to them. You'll automatically have selvedges on both ends.

Quilt 14:
Sweet Dreams

Alice Allen's easy scrap quilt, "Sweet Dreams" (see color section, Figure 24), was assembled on the serger and quilted on the sewing machine. Although it lends itself well to serging, "Sweet Dreams" would look just the same if it were constructed entirely on a regular sewing machine. Alice chose pink, green, and blue for her palette—excellent colors for a baby quilt if the baby's

Figure 15-3. "Sweet Dreams" (detail).

sex is not yet known. (Remember when nobody knew until the baby actually made its premiere appearance?)

"Sweet Dreams" uses two alternating blocks—a four-patch and a sort of rectangular two-patch. Two borders finish it off. Here's how Alice made this quilt. Her sample measures 48″ × 61″, but the design lends itself well to larger or smaller sizes—just add or subtract a row or two.

Materials

$\frac{1}{2}$- to $\frac{3}{4}$-yard cuts or scraps of three pink prints or solids and three blue or green prints or solids, about 3 yards backing fabric (Sweet Dreams is backed with one of the pink prints), one 48″ × 61″ piece of low-loft polyester batting, 50-weight polyester serging thread, regular sewing thread to match backing fabric, extra-fine nylon thread for machine quilting

Tools

Sewing machine, serger, rotary cutter and mat

Directions

1. Wash and dry fabrics; press if needed.

2. Cut borders first. Cut one of the green prints into $1\frac{3}{8}$″-wide strips, equaling 192″ in length. Cut one of the pink prints into strips $2\frac{3}{4}$″ wide, totaling 210″ in length. (Cut a few inches extra for both border sets; your measurements may vary.) Don't piece border strips together yet; set aside.

3. Cut remaining pink, green, and blue fabrics into strips $2\frac{1}{2}$″ wide. If you're using new yardage, cut across the width of the fabric. If you're using scraps, cut crosswise or lengthwise, whichever will give you the longer strips.

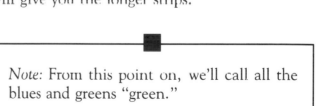

Note: From this point on, we'll call all the blues and greens "green."

4. Set up your serger for a three-thread overlock stitch. Use thread to match fabrics, or any color

that does not contrast strongly. All serger threads will be invisible when quilt is completed. All seams will be ¼"; put needle in left position. Serge all the strips together in pairs, randomly. Serge any pink to any green.

5. Press seams to whichever side seems less visible.

6. For the vertical sets (the blocks consisting of two rectangles), cut segments of green/pink strips 4⅜" long. You'll need about 77 of these.

7. For the four-patches, cut segments of green/pink strips 2½" long; assemble these in pairs to form square four-patch blocks. You'll need about 77 to 80 of these.

8. Arrange 11 alternating blocks together for the first (horizontal) row, beginning with either a vertical set or a four-patch and ending with the same.

9. Arrange the second row. If you began the first row with a vertical set, begin the second row with a four-patch block. To form a secondary pattern, let one of the rectangle colors adjoin that same color in a four-patch block.

10. Serge all the units in the first row together; press seams in one direction. Serge the next row together; press in the opposite direction. Continue until you've serged and pressed 14 rows.

11. Serge rows together in pairs, finger-pressing all seams down as you come to them. Serge pairs together to complete quilt top (except for borders).

12. Piece first border if necessary; serge narrow green strips to quilt top and bottom, then to sides.

13. For an accent for second border, serge in a segment of leftover strip piecing. Serge wider pink strips to quilt top and bottom, then to sides.

14. Press completed quilt top and check for any errors in placement. If you need to remove any stitching, cut threads with seam ripper on one side; then pull thread out and restitch.

15. Cut batting and backing fabric to match size of completed quilt top. Baste or pin-baste quilt layers together.

16. Thread sewing machine with clear nylon thread; use regular sewing thread in bobbin. If you have an even-feed or walking foot, put it on your machine. Machine quilt in the ditch around each four-patch or vertical-set block.

17. Bind quilt, following directions in Chapter 4, "Putting It All Together." Alice's quilt is bound with straight strips of one of the pink fabrics, using the method described for beginning and ending at corners.

Butterfly Squiggles

Have you ever done something for the first time, had it work fine, and then found out you'd done it all wrong? I love it when that happens.

I bought this butterfly fabric years ago. I had no idea what I would do with it, but I just was unable to leave it in the store. Late one night the concept of free-motion quilting flitted across my mind, and I went out to the studio to see whether I had an even-feed foot. I picked up my *Know Your Whatever* book and read therein. (I have three different brands of sewing machines.) Oh joy! The book said you don't need an even-feed foot for free-motion quilting, and I did have the foot I needed—a round one, called a darning foot. I put it on, made me a scrap-batting-scrap sandwich, and went to work. I just dropped the feed dogs (those little metal teeth that move the fabric under the needle) and stuck about four safety pins through my 12" × 20" sandwich. I outlined the leaves printed on the fabric. This was fun! It looked great! Figure 15-5 shows the reverse side.

Now I knew what to do with that butterfly print. I got a good night's sleep, then sandwiched the print with high-loft batting and some nice Concord 100% white cotton fabric. I put the safety pins into the butterfly part of the print, because I'd decided to do all the squiggle quilting

Figure 15-4. "Butterfly Squiggles" (detail). (Photograph by author.)

in the background. This, I reasoned, would make the butterflies raised and puffy and more predominant. I used white thread top and bottom and started doodling around in the middle. See Figure 18 in the color section.

First I outlined all the butterflies. Then,

again starting in the middle, I repeated that line. This is called echo quilting; you echo the shape. Of course, like an auditory echo, it changes and distorts. Then, in between those echo lines, I just squiggled.

When your feed dogs are lowered, you com-

Figure 15-5. The wrong side of a practice piece can look pretty interesting.

pletely control the direction the fabric goes, as well as the stitch length. This gives you a phenomenal amount of freedom. I think you'll enjoy this technique a lot. I did—and I wasn't even doing it right. This piece turned out just like I'd envisioned it. There isn't a pucker anywhere; those layers just clung together like magic.

After the quilt was completed, I found my copy of Robbie and Tony Fanning's *The Complete Book of Machine Quilting*. Ah, yes, consult the authority after the deed is done. Robbie did advise choosing a flower print for practice and outlining the design elements, just as I'd done. She also advised using a larger needle size than you normally would (this had never occurred to me) and said to work in a hoop. A hoop! What a radical concept! I read on: "You can also free-machine quilt without a hoop, but it takes lots of experience to do it well." I guess 30 minutes could be considered lots of experience. "Baste well," directed Robbie. Baste? Another idea that hadn't formed. Well, maybe my safety pins could count as basting.

The point is, it worked. Don't take chances, though. Do it Robbie's way, as outlined below.

Drop or cover feed dogs. Set stitch length and width at 0. Put in a new needle in a slightly larger size than you'd normally use on the fabric of your choice. Loosen top tension a little bit. Practice on a print-scrap–batting–scrap sandwich placed in a hoop, following the design lines on your print (quilt over outer hoop first, then inner ring pressed into place). Begin by drawing up the bobbin thread and holding both threads aside. When you're ready to make your "real" squiggle-quilted piece, baste the layers together.

Specific directions for my Butterfly Squiggles quilt follow.

Materials

Piece of printed fabric about 40″ × 42″, piece of high-loft batting slightly larger than the piece of print fabric, backing fabric the same size as batting, sewing thread (lots of it), about ½ yard of binding fabric of your choice (I used white silk satin for a special touch)

Tools

Scissors, sewing machine with darning foot, embroidery hoop

Directions

1. Wash and dry fabrics; press if needed. Layer top fabric, batting, and backing. Baste.

2. Set machine for free-motion embroidery and thread machine with top thread color to match top fabric and bobbin thread to match backing fabric. This is arbitrary, of course. The back side will look good if your bobbin thread is a contrasting color, too.

3. Put area to be quilted (choose one near the center) in a hoop; place under needle. Bring bobbin thread up; lower presser foot lever. Outline main motifs in hoop area.

4. Move hoop to another area; outline motifs in that area. Continue until all major design elements are outlined.

5. Now move hoop back to center and work as much detailed squiggle quilting as you like. Move hoop to another area and do squiggle quilting. When you move hoop, check back of work to make sure there are no puckers.

6. When piece is all quilted, trim all edges evenly and bind as explained in Chapter 4, "Putting It All Together."

More Ideas in Motion

Once you've experienced the absolute joy and improvisational thrill of free-motion machine quilting, you'll probably want more of the same. Your forays into the fabric store may result in prints you might have overlooked before.

Figure 15-6. Free-motion possibilities. (Photograph by author.)

"Wow," you may think, "That'd be fun to outline." Here are some additional ideas for your free-stitching pleasure:

- Consider the "wrong" side of the quilt as the "right" side. Use a contrasting color of thread in the bobbin and work a bit more carefully.

- Wind a thread onto your bobbin that wouldn't fit through the needle—pearl cotton, perhaps, or a narrow ribbon like Flexi-Braid. Adjust the tension until you're happy with the look of the stitches on the back of the quilt. Depending on how you like the finished effect, you might want to consider the wrong side as the right side.

- Instead of following a printed-fabric design, use solid-color fabric (or perhaps a wide stripe) and write messages or draw freehand pictures. OK, I heard that wimpy "I'm no artist" reply coming from somebody. Actually, people who are not at all proud of their lines on paper are frequently very pleased with their lines on fabric. Maybe that's because we've seen "real" art, and our standards are stricter when the lines are drawn on paper. Maybe there are more reasons. At any rate, give it a try.

- Combine free-motion stitchery with some of the ideas in the section on the "Baby's Big Brother" quilt. Let a child do the drawing on the sewing machine. Even a very young child can do this if you hold him or her in your lap. A child might not be able to manage the whole quilt sandwich, so think about letting him just "squiggle" on one thickness of fabric, then turn that artwork into a block for the quilt.

- Set your machine for zigzag stitching and experiment with free-motion work and a zigzag stitch. It's a whole new look.

Another idea to try is chicken-scratch embroidery stitches on gingham. Instead of just squiggling or writing after you've set up your machine for free-motion stitching, you can duplicate these easy stitches. (Traditional chicken scratch, or Teneriffe, is explained in Chapter 14 in the section called "Going for Gingham.")

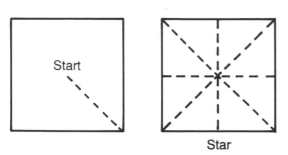

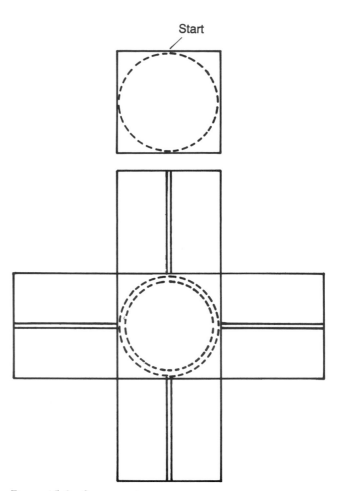

Figure 15-7. *Chicken scratch on the sewing machine.*

Thread needle with dark thread to match gingham and place needle in center of white square. Bring up bobbin thread. Sew from center out to corner, back to center, out to next corner, back to center, and so on, as shown in Figure 15-7. That makes a star, or double cross-stitch. Spokes and wheels are made in one step, as shown in Figure 15-8. Begin stitching at top center of circle. Stitch all the way around the circle. Go around the circle again, this time stopping at each midpoint and making a long straight stitch across the adjacent square to make a spoke. Although the illustration shows the two lines of stitching, you should try to get your second line of stitches right on top of the first. Your stitches probably won't make a perfect circle as sketched, but they won't look bad, either. As you get to each midpoint of the square, make a long straight stitch across the adjoining square, then go back to stitching the circle.

Figure 15-8. *Start at top center.*

CHAPTER SIXTEEN

BONUS QUILT: POCKET PALS

This is the cutest pocket quilt I've ever seen. It is the creation of Janet Sylvain, who calls her quilting business Pieced on Earth. (That's also one of my favorite company names.) If you're counting, this is quilt 15, which makes it a bonus quilt. "Pocket Pals" didn't seem to fit in any of our categories, so it gets its own pocket in this book.

I really admire Janet's work and am delighted to be able to share this impressive yet easy quilt with you. Janet's original name for this quilt is "Critter Quilt," so when we mention critters, you'll know that we mean the little animals that are tucked into the pockets (see color section, Figure 19). Janet's address is listed at the end of this book in Sources of Supply; she makes custom

Figure 16-1. "Pocket Pals" (detail). (Photograph courtesy of PSC Publications.)

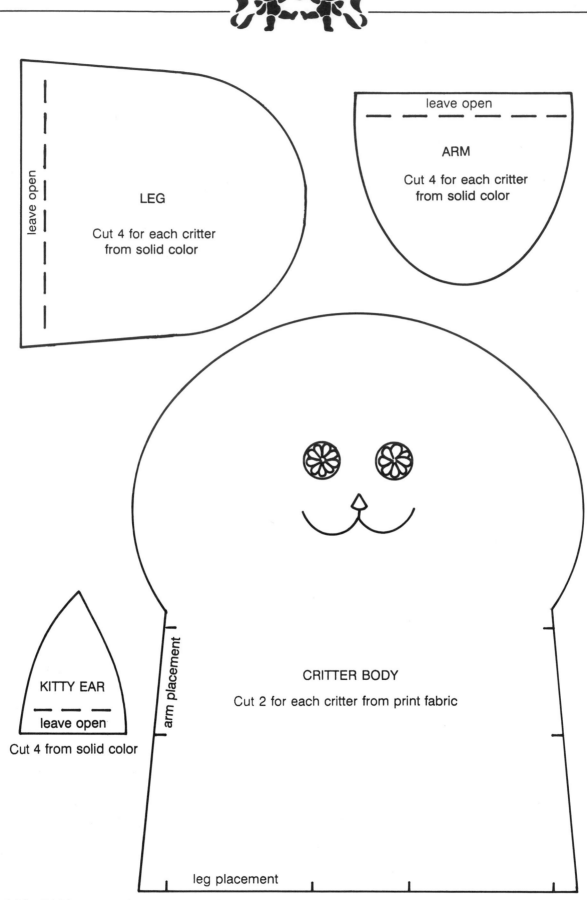

LEG

Cut 4 for each critter
from solid color

leave open

ARM

Cut 4 for each critter
from solid color

leave open

KITTY EAR

leave open

Cut 4 from solid color

arm placement

CRITTER BODY

Cut 2 for each critter from print fabric

leg placement

Figure 16-2. Critter patterns.

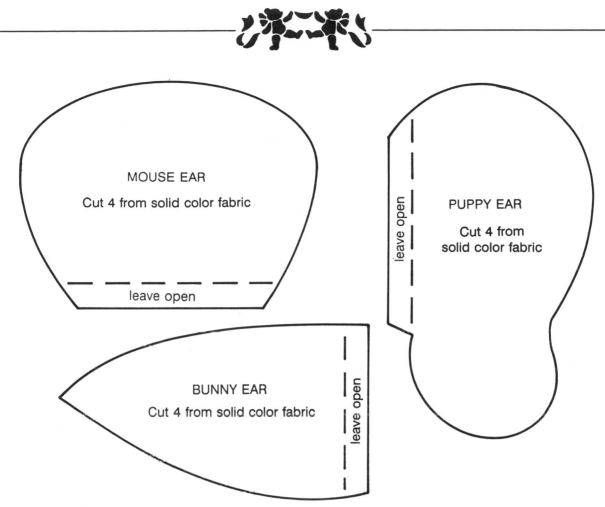

MOUSE EAR

Cut 4 from solid color fabric

leave open

PUPPY EAR

Cut 4 from
solid color fabric

leave open

BUNNY EAR

Cut 4 from solid color fabric

leave open

Figure 16-2 continued. Critter patterns.

quilts. Janet told me in her last letter that she'd just completed five Ultrasuede quilts for a three-bedroom yacht.

Materials

45″-wide cotton fabrics as follows: $\frac{1}{4}$ yard each of yellow print, red print, green print, and blue print; $\frac{1}{3}$ yard each of solid yellow, solid red, and solid blue; 2 yards of solid green; about $\frac{1}{2}$ yard of ribbon for each critter; embroidery floss in black, pink, blue, and green; piece of bonded polyester batting about 42″ × 45″; polyester stuffing for critters; sewing thread to match fabrics

Tools

Sewing machine, scissors or rotary cutter and mat (both would be helpful)

Directions

Wash, dry, and press all fabrics.

Critters

1. Cut out critter pattern pieces from the fabrics shown on patterns (see Figure 16-2). Sew 2 arm pieces together with right sides facing. Make $\frac{1}{4}$″ seams on all steps of sewing critters. Leave the straight edge open. Clip curves and turn right side out.

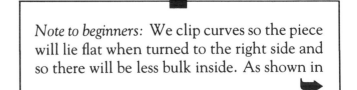

Note to beginners: We clip curves so the piece will lie flat when turned to the right side and so there will be less bulk inside. As shown in

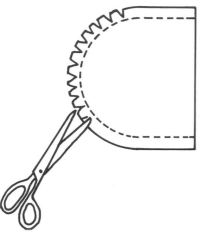

Figure 16-3. Clipping curves.

Figure 16-3, just cut little triangles out of the seam allowance in the curved areas (or use pinking shears). Be careful that you don't clip into the stitching. If you do, just re-stitch—making critters isn't a precision science anyway.

2. Press, then baste the open edges closed and gather the stitching slightly. Sew all arms, legs, and ears this way. Pin to right side of body piece as shown in Figure 16-4. Baste in place.

3. Pin body pieces right sides together (with

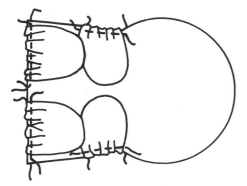

Figure 16-4. Baste arms and legs to body.

basted arms, legs, and ears sandwiched inside). Stitch, leaving about 2″ open at the bottom. Turn right side out and stuff body. Slipstitch the opening closed, or stitch it on the machine. Embroider the faces and tie ribbons around each critter's neck.

Pockets

1. Cut eight $6\frac{1}{2}$″ squares, one from each solid-color fabric and one from each print. Cut a $2\frac{1}{2}$″ square and a strip 1″ × 22″ from each print. From each solid-color fabric, cut a rectangle 11″ × $12\frac{1}{2}$″.

2. Press under $\frac{1}{4}$″ along both edges of the 22″ strips. (Strips will now be $\frac{1}{2}$″ wide.) Pin each strip to a contrasting solid-color $6\frac{1}{2}$″ square, leaving a 1″ solid-color border. Stitch both sides of strip to square, folding in the corners at a diagonal.

Note to beginners: This is called mitering the corners. You'll come across this term often in reading about making quilts. Figure 16-5 shows the principle of mitering; for this quilt, though, the edges of your strip will be pressed under, and you won't need to trim the corner off if you don't want to.

3. Satin-stitch the small square in the center, set on point to form a diamond (see Figure 16-6).

4. Pin pocket to harmonizing print square, right sides together. Stitch, leaving a 2″ opening. Clip corners, turn right side out, and press. Stitch opening closed.

5. Place pocket top on matching solid rectangle, right side up, with a 2″ border on sides and bottom. Topstitch in place along sides and bottom, reinforcing at top corners as shown in Figure 16-6.

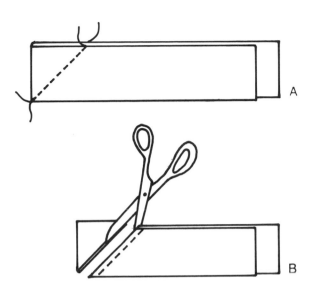

A

B

Quilt Top

1. Use $\frac{3}{8}''$ seams to sew quilt together. Cut 6 strips of red print $2\frac{1}{4}'' \times 12\frac{1}{2}''$. Sew these to the sides of the pocket rectangles (see Figure 16-7).

2. Cut 6 strips from red print $2\frac{1}{4}'' \times 11''$. Cut nine $2\frac{1}{4}''$ squares from blue print. Sew 3 sets of square-strip-square-strip-square. Sew these pieced strips to top, middle, and bottom of pocket panels (Figure 16-8).

3. Cut 2 strips of blue print $2\frac{1}{4}'' \times 25\frac{1}{2}''$; sew to top and bottom of quilt. Cut 2 strips of blue print $2\frac{1}{4}'' \times 32\frac{1}{2}''$; sew to sides of quilt.

4. Cut 2 strips of yellow print $1\frac{3}{4}'' \times 28\frac{1}{2}''$; sew to

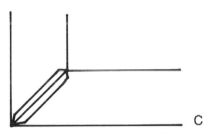

C

Figure 16-5. The basic technique of mitering. A. Stitch at a 45-degree angle. B. Cut off corner. C. Open out seam; press.

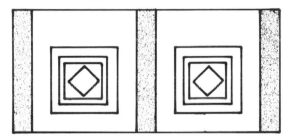

Figure 16-7.

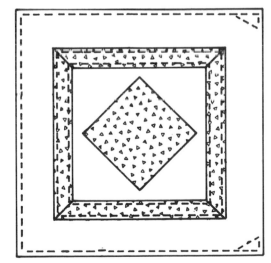

Figure 16-6.

Figure 16-8.

top and bottom of quilt. Cut 2 strips of yellow print $1\frac{3}{4}'' \times 34\frac{1}{2}''$; sew to sides of quilt.

5. Cut 2 strips green print $2\frac{1}{4}'' \times 31''$; sew to top and bottom of quilt. Cut 2 strips green print $2\frac{1}{4}'' \times 37\frac{1}{2}''$; sew to sides.

6. Cut 2 strips red print $2\frac{1}{2}'' \times 34''$; sew to top and bottom of quilt. Cut 2 strips red print $2\frac{1}{4}'' \times 37\frac{1}{2}''$ and 4 blue print $2\frac{1}{4}''$ squares. Piece squares to both ends of both strips. Sew strips to quilt sides.

7. Trim batting to $42'' \times 44\frac{1}{2}''$. Cut solid green backing to $45'' \times 48''$. Place backing on floor, wrong side up, and place batting and quilt top on backing. Pin layers together.

8. Fold backing fabric over batting and raw edges of quilt to form a self-binding around the quilt. Pin the binding; then topstitch, mitering the corners.

9. Tie quilt with yarn, or quilt by hand or machine around seam lines and pockets. Place critters in pockets.

CHAPTER SEVENTEEN
IDEAS FOR BABY'S WALLS

"Just what this apartment needs," moaned Marinda Stewart, "more tchotchkes." Charlie and I are Texans; we'd never heard that word before, but we knew we liked it. "Knick-knacks, little decorative items," Marinda explained. *Tchotchke* rhymes, according to Leo Rosten in *The Joys of Yiddish*, with "botch-a." It comes from a Slavic word meaning "to play pranks." In addition to attributing seven other meanings (including "a sexy but brainless broad") to this delightful word, Mr. Rosten defines *tchotchkes* as toys, playthings, or trinkets.

So—not only is tchotchke one of my all-time favorite words, but tchotchkes are one of the best ways to decorate a wall quilt for baby. Just consider all the things you could tie on, sew on, or even glue on—little toys that could be taken off for play as the baby gets older, squeakers, rattles, bells, buttons, beads, sticks, and stones even. (But read the section called "Safety Specs" in Chapter 19.)

"Dinosaur Parade" was designed for touch and use, with all its textures, but it would make a great wall quilt with even more embellishment, perhaps toy dinosaurs. Meryl Ann Butler's Guardian Angel quilt in Chapter 19 (and color Figure 20) is obviously a wall piece. Check out "Soft Stars" and "Soft Hearts," shown in the color section (Figures 21 and 22) for more starting points for wall quilts. "Soft Stars" uses both woven and tricot-backed lamé, along with star-shaped buttons, sew-on rhinestones, and acrylic jewels. "Soft Hearts" features three layers of lightly padded hearts, each cut a little smaller than the next, all stacked together and tied in

place with Flexi-Braid through a heart-shaped button. Now you wouldn't want to use most of these elements in an everyday quilt (although the padded hearts would work just fine). For wall quilts, though, they're perfect. Full-sized patterns for the heart and the star are given here, and construction technique is the same for both. (Use the faced appliqué method described in Chapter 13, "Appliqué Today.")

Here are some more ideas for wall quilts:

1. Cut out simple shapes from half of a potato to make a stamp. Stars and hearts, again, are good. So are circles, triangles, squares, sunbursts, and squiggles. Dip the cut surface into acrylic paint or any of the many fabric paints on the market; stamp on fabric.

2. Dampen household sponges, then cut into different shapes. Dip sponge into acrylic paint or a

Figure 17-1. Star pattern. Use solid line for cutting, take ¼″ seam; or cut ¼″ outside solid line, then use solid line for stitching.

Figure 17-2. Use solid line for cutting, take ¼″ seam; or cut ¼″ outside solid line, then use solid line for stitching.

special fabric paint; stamp on fabric. You can do a Trip Around the World design with just one square sponge in half an hour! Or *try* stamping this pattern on walls.

3. Cut ribbon into fairly long lengths; stitch the center of each to quilt, and tie in bows. Leave long streamers, if you like, and tie big beads to the ends.

4. Make a "pearlie" quilt. Get out your entire button jar and sew the collection, either in a planned pattern or a random sprinkling, onto the quilt.

5. Stencil the baby's name, other messages, and other shapes onto the quilt. There are lots of precut stencils available and many different paints. If you don't want to go to the store, you can cut your own stencils and use common acrylic paints, slightly diluted with water.

6. Sew on individual sequins, pre-strung sequins, or some of the ready-made sequin appliqués available. *Hint:* Instead of sewing the appliqués to the quilt, sew a tab of Velcro to each. Then you can remove the appliqués for laundering.

7. Decorate with shisha mirrors. One good way

to attach these little bits of glamour is with plastic rings. You may see these called "bone" rings in the stores, but they're still plastic. Here's how the late, beloved Jerry Zarbaugh of Aardvark Adventures taught me to work with them. Choose a ring about the same size in diameter as the mirror. Cover the ring with buttonhole stitches in embroidery floss, rayon thread, or whatever you like. Place the covered ring over the mirror and hold in place with a few hand stitches. This method works only with the round mirrors, of course. For the other shapes, you'll have to attach them with embroidery stitches.

8. Zigzag stitch over lengths of yarn, either in an all-over random pattern, or in lines on blocks. Set machine for a zigzag that will catch the yarn without covering it up.

CHAPTER EIGHTEEN

CARING FOR YOUR QUILT

It's always *your* quilt, even after you give it away. So let's think about some principles of reasonable care and conservation, remembering that this isn't a museum piece. In a sense, we want these quilts to be used up; we just want it to take awhile.

There's a danger in telling the new mother too much about quilt care—she might put the quilt away to keep it "nice." Just tell her not to overclean the quilt. I've given quilts to babies whose mothers threw them (the quilts, not the babies) into the washer and dryer every single week. This is not necessary, of course, and we older mothers know that. New mothers don't, however. They think that everything within 15 feet of little Michelle must be disinfected on a regular basis. The result of all this zeal, of course, is that you must construct an industrial-strength quilt.

I like to offer a free repair service. We've already talked about offering to replace quilt bindings, especially my favorite, red satin. The binding will wear out in a year or two, so tell the parents you know that the binding is going to wear out and that when it does, you'll replace it. Tell them, too, that you'll make emergency repairs to the quilt. Otherwise, they'll be embarrassed to tell you that little Matthew carried it out into the yard to make a tent, and the dog chewed a hole in it. This sort of disaster doesn't upset a quilter; it pleases her, because it says the kid is enjoying the quilt. Convey this perspective to the new parents in as few words as you can—maybe in a letter, sent after the actual gift-giving of the quilt.

We've danced around this long enough: Tell

remove the dubious embellishments (buttons and beads, of course, are eminently washable) and hand wash the rest. Of course any quilt will last longer and retain brighter colors with this kind care.

Here's a short course in hand washing a quilt. With slight adjustments, these instructions will save you billions of dollars in dry-cleaning charges, because they're also directions for washing your silk blouses. (Of course, for smaller items substitute the bathroom sink for the bathtub.)

Look at the quilt carefully all over; make any needed repairs before laundering. Now run a generous amount of warmish water into tub, along with a stingy bit of special quilt detergent like Ensure™ Quilt Wash, dishwashing detergent, or even shampoo. Put the quilt into the water and lightly swish it around a time or two, pushing it under or through the water but not pulling it at all. Go have a cup of tea and think about your next quilt design. Swish the quilt around again. If you noticed any specially dirty areas, you can rub them, but not too hard. If the quilt is very dirty, let the water run out of the tub, push the quilt into the end of the tub, and refill with the mix of warm water and detergent. Swish and soak again. If quilt is very, very dirty and sewn together strongly, get into the tub barefoot and walk around on it. This provides a good foot massage and a good way to wash things.

When the quilt is clean enough to suit you, push it to the back of the tub, let the water run out, and refill the tub with warmish or coolish water. Swish quilt around pretty good. Push to back of tub; drain. Refill tub, this time adding a splash (between a tablespoon and $\frac{1}{4}$ cup) of common household white vinegar. The vinegar will cut through any detergent residue and make the colors sparkle. If you walked on the quilt before, walk on it again.

OK, this is the only tricky part. A wet quilt is delicate; all those cellulose or protein fibers are weaker when wet. So you want to lift the quilt as

Figure 18-1. Beth Hayes takes good care of the doll quilt she designed.

the parents the quilt can be machine washed and dried, but that they should not overdo it. That's really the best you can do. If, as in the case of a wall hanging with charms and tchotchkes hanging from it, the piece can *not* be machine washed, it would be nice of you to offer a cleaning service, as well. The bright side of this is that such a quilt shouldn't require cleaning more than once or twice in its lifetime. And all you'll do then is

gently as possible, all at once. Squeeze as much water out of the quilt as you can, but don't twist it or wring it out. This is a good time to walk gently on the quilt, because it's an easy way to press the water out toward the drain.

Pick up the quilt in one mound and lay it in a basket containing a big dry towel or a sheet. Squeeze more water out; repeat with another towel if you want. (The wet quilt is still in a lump or mound at this point). Lay quilt out to dry flat on a sheltered surface padded with an old blanket, old towels, or whatever. Car trunks or hoods are usually flat enough for this purpose; picnic tables are good; so are empty pickup-truck beds. You can let the bright sun shine on the quilt for 10 minutes, but any longer may fade the colors.

Most user-friendly baby quilts can be machine washed and dried, but the kind hand treatment described above will prolong their lives. You could offer to do this treatment once a year, perhaps on the child's birthday. Of course, the child might not be able to do without his or her beloved quilt for the few days such a washing might require.

CHAPTER NINETEEN
PICKING UP THE PIECES

Just as in finishing up a quilt you'll find lots of leftover patches and trims that didn't fit into the quilt but seem somehow to belong and are definitely too valuable to discard, in finishing a book, the same thing happens. When you're making a quilt, you have several options. You can put the coordinated scrap elements into a shoe box, label it "Tony's Quilt" or whatever, and know that box contains those bits and pieces; you can refile the leftover things; you can make a pillow to match the quilt. In books, the easiest thing to do is to add a soup-pot chapter, and that's what this chapter is. We'll talk about safety, books about quilts, combining quilt techniques, and quilts for needy children. We'll listen to a few well-chosen words from quilters and other craftspeople, and we'll take a look at a very special quilt, Meryl Ann Butler's "Guardian Angel."

I have items on my personal agenda that will have to fit here, too. If you want to write to me, or order an autographed copy of *The Fabric Lover's Scrapbook,* or send me some red scraps for my ongoing charm-quilt project, please do so. My address is included in Sources of Supply at the end of this book.

Combinations

Once you've learned how to make a lemon pie and a coconut pie, you can probably make a lemon-coconut pie. So, too, can you combine bits and pieces from techniques explained in this

book to make your own individual creations. For example:

- Combine simple checkerboard patchwork with appliqué. Stitch hearts or flowers in the open areas of an Irish chain pattern.
- Start your Log Cabin block with a little nine-patch instead of a solid-color square.
- Use the machine-tying method described in Chapter 4, "Putting It All Together," to make the tied gingham quilt, "Check It Out," from Chapter 14.
- Add a randomly strip-pieced border to a checkerboard or striped center. Such a border might provide just the needed visual interest.
- Use the pocket-quilt concept (Pocket Pals, Chapter 16), but use pockets from jeans and denim squares and/or substitute other toys, either handmade or store-bought.

Safety Specs

We all have good sense, so this will be a short section. We are making things for little babies, though, and it won't hurt us to take a refresher course in kid and baby safety.

The section on wall quilts describes techniques and embellishments that break many of these rules. If you decide to make a wall quilt with these "iffy" ingredients, you must make absolutely certain that the parents are mature and wise—that is, that they won't decide to toss the buttons-and-beads wall hanging onto the floor just once to let the baby feel it. Still, let's be reasonable. Even if you abstain from sewing buttons on your wall quilt, that is no guarantee that the baby's two-year-old sister won't feed him buttons anyway.

I would strongly advise against using the following ingredients in baby quilts (except on wall quilts):

- Fabric paint
- Fabric dye
- Buttons
- Beads
- Squeaker toys
- Musical inserts
- Rhinestones
- Acrylic jewels
- Loose ribbons

When I made my all-corduroy quilt called "New Bluebird," I intended it to be for a baby. But I got so carried away with using up all my corduroy scraps that I sewed little belt-loop-like narrow bands over the seam lines. These little bands are great fun for eyes and fingers, and I'd feel fine seeing this quilt in the hands of a healthy three-year-old. But I kept having vague worries about baby hands or feet getting twisted into the bands, so I kept it. (Besides, I like the quilt, and no one else has ever indicated any affection for it.) So to good sense, don't be afraid to add intuition. If it crosses your mind that a quilt treatment might be dangerous, don't do it. Better

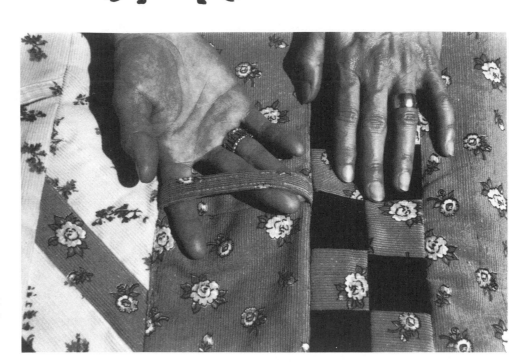

Figure 19-1. I worried about baby feet getting tangled in these loops, so I kept "New Bluebird" for myself.

yet, do it for yourself just for fun, and make the baby a safe substitute.

I was enormously surprised to hear that lint from frayed fabrics can be hazardous to baby's lungs. Two of my original fourteen quilts were intended to be made in different slash-and-fray techniques. My reasoning was purely sensual: The baby would nestle into a cloudlike pillow of yards of soft-edged cut fabric strips.

One of the techniques was developed by a Minnesota fiber artist, Tim Harding, whose wearables and home-dec pieces are nationally recognized. I called Mr. Harding to ask his permission to adapt his method for a baby quilt and was met with strong resistance—not to my borrowing the art form, but to its use for little babies. Both the artist and his assistant warned me that the large quantity of lint produced could be harmful.

Because of these warnings, I re-planned the line up and designed the "Pink Cloud" quilt as a substitute, feeling that the serged edges would prevent lint buildup. Still, if I were making a quilt for a healthy toddler, I think I'd consider using

frayed fabric. After all, haven't we all laid babies on chenille bedspreads?

Note, too, that the "Dinosaur Parade" quilt has a small amount of frayed appliqué. Bottom line: common sense. Don't give a frayed-fabric quilt to a newborn or a baby who has any respiratory difficulty.

Books for Kids

Here are some children's books that focus on quilts. One of these books might make a good follow-up or tandem gift for a child who's also receiving a quilt from you.

- *The Patchwork Quilt* by Valerie Flournoy, with pictures by Jerry Pinkney, tells the story of a young black girl and her grandmother, time and love, and the quilt they make together. It's my current favorite. (E.P. Dutton, Inc., Dial Books for Young Readers, New York, 1985)

- *The Quilt* by Ann Jones is mostly the story of a little girl's dream. She falls asleep under a new

quilt made for her by her mother and father (!) out of scraps of memory-laden fabric. Little text, mostly pictures. (Greenwillow Books, New York, 1984)

- *The Keeping Quilt* by Patricia Polacco traces the history of an appliquéd quilt through several generations of her family while illustrating the rich traditions of Russian Jews. (Simon and Schuster Books for Young Readers, New York, 1988)

- *Patchwork Tales* by Susan L. Roth and Ruth Phang uses a sampler quilt as a basis for a grandmother's stories. (Atheneum, New York, 1984)

- *The Berenstain Bears and Mama's New Job* by Stan and Jan Berenstain has a slant on sexual politics as well as on business and art. Mama's expression is priceless when Papa pats her on the shoulder and says, "Mama in business? I don't think so. One business-bear in the family is enough." I wish I had grandchildren so I could read this to them. (Random House, New York, 1984)

A Letter from Beth

When my pen pal Beth Swider heard that I was working on a book about baby quilts, she took pen in hand. Beth is the same woman who read *Fabric Lover's Scrapbook* and sent me pictures of several rooms in her house where she had put those ideas into practice—from the living room walls to the bathroom mirror. Beth doesn't just read and dream, she by golly goes out and *does it!* So I was delighted, but not really surprised, to read the following letter from her. Just read along with me:

I *love* making baby quilts, and I have some ideas to share in case you're running out.

Once I made a baby quilt for a friend who loved sheep. So at the very top of the quilt, I had a large sheep standing by a fence with a cartoon-type bubble coming out of her mouth saying, "Welcome to the flock!" This sheep was standing on some grass that, if you looked carefully, spelled out her name—that of the oldest grand aunt of the family of the baby-to-be. Below the auntie sheep, in the meadow, were "families" of sheep. Each sheep had its name written in the grass below it. Flowers dotted the i's, and every once in a while, I'd write things like Rota, Spain (the place where the baby was to be born), and silly love words and phrases here and there.

Another quilt I made in Spain used the usual animals and numbers, but I noted each in Spanish.

One friend loved koala bears, so my daughter drew a mother and baby koala, and I centered the drawing and surrounded the bears with leaves. At the shower, each guest signed a leaf. After the shower, I machine embroidered over their signatures. The gift was not only a beautiful quilt, but also a remembrance of the fun we had at the shower.

Another friend was partial to unicorns, and for her, my daughter drew a mother and baby unicorn. I surrounded them with hearts, the guests each signed a heart, and I used yarn stitchery to embroider the names.

One friend was an artist herself, so I used a duck she had drawn. I placed the duck in a puddle that spelled out Baby Reed (the family's last name). The duck was looking up to the cloudy sky as raindrops were falling. At her shower, the guests signed their names in the clouds.

I made a quilt with a lighthouse and one with a sailboat; in each design, I spelled out the recipient's name in the waves of the sea.

How about making a "handsome" quilt? Each guest at the shower could sign a handprint with her name. And speaking of names, why not use nautical flags to spell out the baby's name? This would be especially

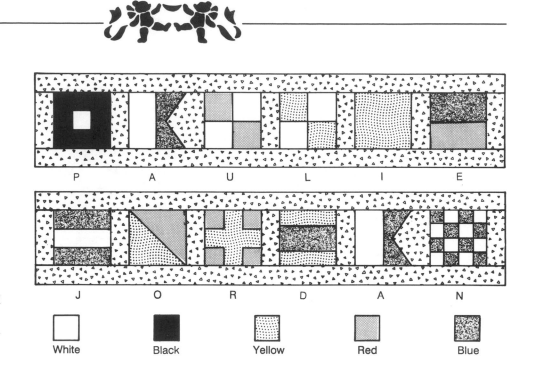

Figure 19-2. Nautical signal flags can be used to spell names, and they add the fun of a "secret" code.

P A U L I E

J O R D A N

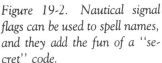

White   Black   Yellow   Red   Blue

good for baby boys. [Most of the letters would be easy to do in patchwork or with bias-tape or ribbon trim. See Figure 19-2.]

A cute quilt could be made showing kittens drinking spilled milk, with the milk puddle spelling out the baby's name. Or a bouquet of flowers could have the baby's name and other important info embroidered on the petals. Or a bear or clown holding balloons could have the names and baby info inside the balloons. Why not a family tree with names on the leaves and family names "carved" into the bark along the various branches?

I just finished two baby quilts for a dear friend's grandchildren. Both used the classic Trip Around the World color arrangement. One of the quilts had signatures of the guests at the little one's first birthday party. These squares were solid color so the messages would be easy to read. Any blank solid was decorated with a simple drawing to keep the balance. The second quilt had only the drawings because, during a move, the mom misplaced the signature squares. Each quilt had the child's name spelled out on it. I used

dowels in the top and bottom hem of one of them so that it could serve as a wallhanging.

Quotes from Quilters

A finished quilt which has no imperfections, artistically or technically, is one which was created within the quilter's comfort zone. No significant learning will [occur] when we stay within this safe place.

—Joen Wolfrom
   from *Quilter's Newsletter*

Sarah Dunn (maker of an early twentieth-century baby quilt in black, red, and green) was willing to say through this quilt to her granddaughter, "I am a strong person. I have ideas. I am not afraid. I can make strong statements. I was here. Know me. I value you. Don't forget me." Likewise I wanted my son to be surrounded by strong shapes and strong colors because I felt his intelligence deserved such strength. I felt he deserved more than cute pinks and blues!

—Nancy Crow
   in *Quilts and Influences*

I . . . think that graphing out every detail of the quilt and then following the diagram to the letter is like putting a soul behind bars. . . . Running out of fabric or space only encourages further creative solutions.

—Cindy Vermillion-Davis
from *Quilter's Newsletter*

These is not art to me, all these squares and things. Real art has, you know, like a madonna in it.

—Anonymous
(written in a guest book at an exhibition of modern art)

How much piecin' a quilt is like livin' a life! Many a time I've set and listened to Parson Page preachin' about predestination and free will, and I've said to myself, "If I could just git up there in the pulpit with one of my quilts, I could make life a heap plainer than parson's makin' it with his big words."

You see, to make a quilt you start out with just so much caliker; you don' go to the store and pick it out and buy it, but the neighbors give you a piece here and there and you'll find you have a piece left over every time you've cut out a dress, and you jest take whatever happens to come. That's the predestination.

But when it comes to cuttin' out the quilt, why, you're free to choose your own pattern. You give the same kind of pieces to two persons and one'll make a nine-patch and the other one'll make a wild-goose chase and so there'll be two quilts made of the same kind of pieces but jest as different as can be. That's the way of livin'. The Lord sends us the pieces; we can cut 'em out and put 'em together pretty much to suit ourselves. There's a heap more in the cuttin' out and the sewin' than there is in the caliker.

—Eliza Calvert Hall
from *Aunt Jane of Kentucky*

All God's Children

You're probably not a whole lot like Mother Teresa; I know I'm not. You're going to make baby quilts for the kids you know and love, and the babies (or grandbabies) of your friends and relatives. That's good, healthy selfishness. But if you run out of recipients before you run out of brilliant ideas and brightly colored fabric, there are plenty of babies and children out there in the world if you still want to make a few more baby quilts.

When my friend Barbara Rothacker heard about this book in progress, she wrote me several similar notes, all telling me to get in touch with the Denton (Texas) Quilt Guild. I communicated with several women of the guild, all enthusiastic about their projects. They provide quilts for several worthy groups—for foster children, for a prenatal clinic for young single mothers, and for the police to carry in their cars. The Foster Parents Association now has a stack of quilts in the office. Each foster child who enters can select his or her own favorite to keep. Many of these children leave their homes with nothing more than the clothes they're wearing. A quilt is a tangible, portable, and comforting item that they can carry with them to whatever arrangement may be next in their uncertain lives. And of course, unlike a factory-made object, a quilt has love and power stitched into it. The women of the guild shared a letter from a foster parent. It said, in part:

Our foster daughter arrived in our home with nothing more than a diaper and a many-sizes-too-big gown. That was it—nothing that was her very own. Her case is not at all unique—most foster children arrive with simply the clothes on their backs. They are confused and frightened and have nothing to hold on to for security and comfort. We hope to be able to adopt our foster daughter and secure her future in our family. However, whatever happens in her life and wherever she goes, her quilt will be with her, and always remain the first thing that was truly hers during a very turbulent time. She will always know who it

came from and the love and concern that is present in each stitch of it.

The fact that over 50 quilts were given to foster children in less than six months is, at the same time, a sad commentary on our society and a testament to the quilters' compassion.

Sometimes the police apprehend a suspect who has a child with him or her. When these unfortunate incidents arise, the police can now offer some small comfort by giving the child a handmade quilt to keep.

A few miles south of Denton, my own area quilt guild regularly supplies quilts to the local children's hospital and women's shelter.

The Methodist Home for Children and Youth in Macon, Georgia, began a quilt project. Says Emory C. Gilbert, director of development for the home, "The first day [the kids] are on the campus, they come to the office and choose from six quilts that we keep displayed there at all times. These are symbols of the love and concern of the people from throughout the South Georgia Conference." From this same home comes the powerful story of a young girl who had suffered severe abuse. She entered the home, but soon it became evident that she needed psychiatric care in a hospital setting. She had chosen her quilt on the first day and had been told that someone cared enough for her, without ever knowing her, to spend hours to make this beautiful quilt. Later, hospital staff told the administrators of the home that the quilt, and the love and compassion it represented, was going to be the key to the girl's recovery.

Ellen Ahlgren is a retired social worker who now counsels people with terminal illnesses, including AIDS. She had made quilts for her own children and grandchildren and decided to initiate a program for giving quilts to babies born with the virus. Says Ellen: "I thought the children would love to have a cozy quilt to wrap up in. These babies have little hope for a quality life experience. Their only chance for unconditional love is from people who are aware and willing to do something." Her ABC Quilts project (AIDS Baby Crib Quilts) is going strong. If you'd like to help, ABC needs volunteers to make crib-sized quilts or to donate fabrics, batting, thread, and money for materials and delivery costs. Write to Ellen at ABC Quilts, Sherburne Hill Road, Northwood, NH 03261.

As with so many of the quotes in this book, I read the following in *Quilter's Newsletter Magazine* (No. 157, Nov/Dec 1983). It's from the *Quilts in Women's Lives* videotape: "Quilts are a unique kind of love, you know. It is good for children to know that someone who did not know them, and who they do not know, wanted them to have a quilt just for being born; not for being good—just for being."

The Guardian Angel

Meryl Ann Butler of Virginia Beach, Virginia, designed and coordinated the first United States–Soviet Children's Peace Quilt Exchange Project. She's been to Russia twice in the role of citizen diplomat, speaking about art and peace. She made the "Guardian Angel" quilt, shown in the color section of this book (Figure 20). It's obviously beautiful in and of itself. The angel, dressed in marbleized silk with jeweled detail, hovers in space, her hand-painted face tranquil, yet powerful. She has a silver halo and white moiré wings and is placed on a pre-quilted background. This angel is one of a series that Meryl's creating—not just for beauty alone, but also as a healing image.

Meryl works on the angels only when she is in a serene and concentrated state. She believes that "the energy that is held in the consciousness flows through into work created by the hands, and remains there to be received by the viewer or owner of the handwork."

Meryl told me the story of one little girl who had been abused in her early childhood; the expe-

rience had left her, years later, suffering from frequent nightmares, insomnia, and crippling fears. The child's mother asked Meryl to make her a guardian angel, which Meryl promptly produced and delivered. Almost overnight, the little girl's most obvious symptoms abated, and the passing weeks saw progressive improvement. The child herself attributed her better feeling to *her* angel and even went so far as to recommend an angel for helping other hurt and troubled children.

There are more powers and mysteries in this world than our intelligences can grasp—and I'm not getting mushy-minded on you. Chat with a physicist about quasars, quarks, and redshifts for a few minutes if you think everything you know will fit neatly into column A or B. Comfort and healing are in short enough supply, so guardian angels are a fine idea in any form you can get them, I say.

Now—don't you want to get started on a baby quilt? I know I do, so let's say so long for now. We'll catch up with each other later, with quilts to share and quilts to spare.

SOURCES OF SUPPLY

Because addresses and prices change from time to time, it would be a good idea, before ordering from the following mail-order companies, to send a letter of inquiry, along with a stamped, self-addressed envelope for reply. Or you could be frivolous and trust that details remain the same.

Aardvark Adventures in Handcrafts, P.O. Box 2449, Livermore, CA 94550. Catalog/newsletter offering shisha mirrors, threads, beads, fabric paints, and news about other needle artists. As we go to press, $2 will get you a sample issue, plus that amount credited to your first order.

American Quilter's Society, P.O. Box 3290, Paducah, KY 42002-3290. Offers members discounts on books; presents annual show. Year's membership fee is $15; write for details.

Beaver Island Quilts, 155 Beaver Island, St. James, MI 49782. Gwen Marston and Joe Cunningham offer quilting workshops each autumn; they fill up early in the year. Gwen and Joe also market their own excellent videotapes on all phases of quiltmaking, and they've written some good books.

Books on Tape, P.O. Box 7900, Newport Beach, CA 92658. Write for catalog of books on tape to buy or rent. You can order quickly with their 800 number.

Cabin Fever Calicoes, P.O. Box 550106, Atlanta, GA 30355. Lots of calicoes indeed; also books and quilting supplies. Catalog is $2.50.

Clotilde, Inc., 1909 S.W. First Ave., Ft. Lauderdale, FL 33315-2100. Mail-order source for sewing notions, quilting supplies, gadgets, threads, books, etc. Good prices, speedy service. Catalog is $2.

Come Quilt With Me, P.O. Box 021063, Brooklyn, NY 11202-0023. Pat Yamin's catalog offers quilting tools, videotapes, and books—lots of good stuff.

Crafts by Claire Field, P.O. Box 2254, Redlands, CA 92373. *Tie It! You'll Like It!* contains directions for several sizes and styles of tied gingham quilts as well as other tied quilts. Book is $8 postpaid. No. 15 needles are eight for $1.25 postpaid. Send a stamped, self-addressed envelope for price list of other supplies.

Crazy Ladies and Friends, 1606 Santa Monica Blvd., Santa Monica, CA 90404. This is Mary Ellen Hopkin's store; stop in and visit. You can also order Mary Ellen's books, her "It's OK" rhinestone pin (without which I hardly feel dressed), quilting tools, and T-shirts.

Dicmar Trading Co., P.O. Box 3533, Georgetown Station, Washington, DC 20007. Marie Carr's catalog, "The Whole Quilting Book List," is available from this address.

Doris Carmack's *Easy Biscuit Quilting* is $5 plus $1.50 postage and handling from Doris at 10841 La Batista Ave., Fountain Valley, CA 92708.

Dover St. Booksellers, 39 E. Dover St., Box 1563, Easton, MD 21601. Carries a complete line of quilting books—over 600 titles! Catalog is $2.

Grass Roots Publishing, 950 Third Ave., New York, NY 10022. Publishers of *Creative Quilting* magazine and marketers of several patterns of cheater cloth, including two styles of alphabets.

Joanne's Creations, P.O. Box 28262, Tempe, AZ 85282. Joanne Allen reviews needlecraft-related books, then sells them at a discount. Not a bad idea!

Kaye Wood Publishing Co., 4949 Rau Road, West Branch, MI 48661. Videotapes and books, quilting supplies, and specialized tools—including a cutout square template.

Keepsake Quilting, Dover St., P.O. Box 1459, Meredith, NH 03253. Notions, books, patterns, and fabrics. Free catalog.

Meryl Ann Butler, maker of the "Guardian Angel" quilt, can be reached by writing to her at 828 Deary Lane, Virginia Beach, VA 23451.

R. & E. Miles, P.O. Box 1916, San Pedro, CA 90733. Source for *Aunt Jane of Kentucky* and other books.

Nancy's Notions, P.O. Box 683, Beaver Dam, WI 53916. Quilting supplies, sewing notions, videotapes, books.

Needlearts International, P.O. Box 6447, Dept. CP2, Glendale, CA 91225. Specializes in sashiko quilting; also books, patterns, stencils, quilt supplies, and imported cotton fabrics—including some pre-pieced (not printed, really pieced) Indian cotton. Pattern for wonderful sashiko confetti baby quilt is only $6. Catalog is $2.

Oliver Press, Box 75277, St. Paul, MN 55175-0277. Write to Jeannie Spears at this address for more information on workshops, *The Professional Quilter* magazine, books, and patterns.

Open Chain Publishing, P.O. Box 2634, Menlo Park, CA 94026. Source for *Singer Instructions for Art Embroidery and Lace Work, The Complete Book of Machine Quilting,* and many others.

Quilting Books Unlimited, 1158 Prairie, Aurora, IL 60506. Large selection of quilt-related books. Catalog is $1.

Quilts & Other Comforts, Box 394-4, 6700 W. 44th Ave., Wheatridge, CO 80034-0394. Patterns, templates, books, kits, and accessories. These are the same people who publish *Quilter's Newsletter Magazine* and *Quiltmaker.* Catalog is $2.50.

Treadleart, 25834 Narbonne Ave., Lomita, CA 90717. Quilting books, sewing notions, and a vast array of items for the stitcher. Catalog is $2.

Note: You can write to the author at P.O. Box 606, Azle, TX 76020. Send 4″ red or red print squares for charm quilts, friendly letters, or orders for autographed copies of *The Fabric Lover's Scrapbook* ($17.00 postpaid).

BOOK LIST

Cooper, Patricia, and Norma Bradley Buferd. *The Quilters—Women and Domestic Art.* Garden City, NY: Doubleday & Co., Inc., 1977.

Crow, Nancy. *Quilts and Influences.* Paducah, KY: American Quilter's Society, 1989.

Fanning, Robbie and Tony. *The Complete Book of Machine Quilting.* Radnor, PA: Chilton Book Company, 1980.

Hall, Eliza Calvert. *Aunt Jane of Kentucky.* Facsimile version published by R. & E. Miles, San Pedro, CA, 1986.

Hargrave, Harriet. *Heirloom Machine Quilting.* Westminster, CA: Burdett Publications, 1987.

Hopkins, Mary Ellen. *The It's Okay If You Sit on My Quilt Book.* Atlanta, GA: Yours Truly, Inc., 1982.

Hopkins, Mary Ellen. *Baker's Dozen Doubled.* Fountain Valley, CA: ME Publications, 1988.

Jerstorp, Karin, and Eva Kohlmark. *The Textile Design Book.* Asheville, NC: Lark Books, 1988.

Johannah, Barbara. *The Quick Quiltmaking Handbook.* Menlo Park, CA: Pride of the Forest, 1979.

Leman, Bonnie, and Louise O. Townsend. *How to Make a Quilt: 25 Easy Lessons for Beginners.* Wheatridge, CO: Moon Over the Mountain Publishing Co., 1971 and 1972.

Leon, Eli. *Who'd A Thought It: Improvisation in African-American Quiltmaking.* San Francisco: San Francisco Craft & Folk Art Museum, 1987.

McClun, Diana, and Laura Nownes. *Quilts! Quilts!! Quilts!!!* San Francisco: The Quilt Digest Press, 1988.

Shaeffer, Claire. *Fabric Sewing Guide.* Radnor, PA: Chilton Book Company, 1989.

Singer Instructions for Art Embroidery and Lace Work. Facsimile version published by Open Chain, Menlo Park, CA, 1989.

Swim, Laurie. *The Joy of Quilting.* Ontario, Canada: Viking, Penguin Books Canada, Inc., 1984.

Wien, Carol Anne. *The Great American Log Cabin Quilt Book.* New York: E.P. Dutton, Inc., 1984.

PUBLICATIONS LIST

Prices change; I'd write for an update.

American Quilter, $15 for a one-year subscription (4 issues) from The American Quilter's Society, 5801 Kentucky Dam Road, Paducah, KY 42001.

Crafts 'n Things, $12 for a one-year subscription (8 issues) from 14 Main St., Park Ridge, IL 60068.

Home Quilt Show, $14.95 for a one-year subscription (6 issues) from Cartwright Publications, P.O. Box 927, 308 N. Tyler, Big Sandy, TX 75755.

Lady's Circle Patchwork Quilts, $14.95 for a one-year subscription (6 issues) from P.O. Box 2039, Knoxville, IA 50197. Sample issue is $3.95 postpaid.

Quilter's Newsletter Magazine, $14.95 for a one-year subscription (10 issues) from Box 394, 6700 West 44th Ave., Wheatridge, CO 80033. Sample issue is $4.45 postpaid.

Quiltmaker, $12.95 for a one-year subscription (4 issues) from Box 394, 6700 West 44th Ave., Wheatridge, CO 80033. Sample issue is $5.20 postpaid.

Sew News, $15.97 for a one-year subscription (12 issues) from P.O. Box 3134, Harlan, IA 51537.

Threads, $22 for a one-year subscription (6 issues) from 63 S. Main Street, Box 355, Newtown, CT 06470.

Index